GW00649934

Investigating Sex

Endpaper illustration: Dora Maar, *Untitled*, *c.* 1932–35, courtesy of Galerie 1900–2000, Paris.

Investigating Sex

Surrealist Research 1928–1932

Edited by
JOSÉ PIERRE

Translated by Malcolm Imrie

With an Afterword by Dawn Ades

VERSO
London · New York

This book has been published with
the financial assistance of the
French Ministry of Culture.

First published as *Recherches sur la sexualité, janvier 1928 – août 1932*
by Gallimard, Paris 1990
This translation first published by Verso 1992

Verso
UK: 6 Meard Street, London W1V 3HR
USA: 29 West 35th Street, New York, NY 10001-2291

Verso is the imprint of New Left Books

ISBN 0-86091-378-3

British Library Cataloguing in Publication Data
A catalogue record for this book is available from the British Library

Library of Congress Cataloging-in-Publication Data
A catalogue record for this book is available from the Library of Congress

Typeset in Ehrhardt by York House Typographic Ltd, London W7
Printed and bound in Great Britain by
Biddles Ltd, Guildford and King's Lynn

Contents

Translator's Note vii

First Session 1

Second Session 19

Third Session 37

Fourth Session 51

Fifth Session 67

Sixth Session 83

Seventh Session 97

Eighth Session 107

Ninth Session 121

Tenth Session 135

Eleventh Session 143

Twelfth Session 149

Appendices 153

I General Observations 155

II Inquiry (1929) 157

III Inquiry (1933) 159

IV An Inquiry into Striptease (1958-59) 163

V An Inquiry into Erotic Representations (1964-65) 165

VI Introduction to the International Surrealist Exhibition (1959) 167

Notes on Participants *by Malcolm Imrie* 173

Afterword *by Dawn Ades* 185

Notes 207

Translator's Note

Several people helped me with the translation, the biographical notes and the picture research: Alastair Brotchie, Liz Heron, Pierre Naville, Donald Nicholson-Smith (who also copy-edited the manuscript), José Pierre, Michael Richardson, Martina Dervis and, above all, Paul Hammond, a one-man compendium of surrealist knowledge.
Thanks a lot.

M.I.

Benjamin Péret and his son Geyser in Paris, 1932.
Photograph by André Thirion. (Collection André Thirion)

*First Session**

27 JANUARY 1928

André Breton

Max Morise

Pierre Naville

Benjamin Péret

Jacques Prévert

Raymond Queneau

Yves Tanguy

Pierre Unik

* The text of this session was published in *La révolution surréaliste*, no. 11 (15 March 1928). The full title was: 'Research into Sexuality/The Place of Objectivity, Individual Determinants, Degree of Consciousness'. The manuscript in the André Breton archives contains some variations from the printed text. These are given within square brackets in the notes at the end of the book, unless they have been deleted in the manuscript (although some deletions – which seemed to merit inclusion – will also be found in the notes).

Trans. Of these variations and additions, I have included in the notes only those which in my opinion alter the sense significantly, and have excluded those which are practically synonymous with the printed text (for example, 'she' instead of 'the woman', or 'Morise, is this your opinion?' instead of 'Is this the opinion of Morise?'). Readers requiring a complete list should refer to the French edition.

ANDRÉ BRETON A man and a woman make love. To what extent is the man aware of the woman's orgasm? Tanguy?

YVES TANGUY Hardly at all.[1]

ANDRÉ BRETON Do you have any objective ways of telling?

YVES TANGUY Yes.

We are not told what these are.

ANDRÉ BRETON What does Queneau think?

RAYMOND QUENEAU There are no ways.

ANDRÉ BRETON Prévert?

JACQUES PRÉVERT It depends on the woman.

ANDRÉ BRETON Do you have objective ways of telling?

JACQUES PRÉVERT Yes, yes, yes, yes.

ANDRÉ BRETON Which?

JACQUES PRÉVERT (*Does not reply.*)

ANDRÉ BRETON Péret?

BENJAMIN PÉRET No way. And Breton?

ANDRÉ BRETON There are only subjective ways, which one can trust to the extent that one can trust the woman in question.

BENJAMIN PÉRET I agree with Breton.

RAYMOND QUENEAU To what extent does Breton trust a woman?

ANDRÉ BRETON To the extent that I love her. Naville, to what extent, etc.?

PIERRE NAVILLE That depends on the woman.

ANDRÉ BRETON In a given case, can you be sure whether she has an orgasm?

PIERRE NAVILLE Yes, certainly.

ANDRÉ BRETON How?

PIERRE NAVILLE Thanks to various illusions of a mental nature.

MAX MORISE If they are recognised to be illusions, they are not objective signs.

PIERRE NAVILLE I do not believe in objective signs.

ANDRÉ BRETON A man and woman make love. To what extent is the woman aware of the man's orgasm? Morise?

MAX MORISE I have absolutely no idea.

ANDRÉ BRETON How can that be?

MAX MORISE Because I have no way of telling.

PIERRE NAVILLE What ways of telling do you think one could have in such a case?

MAX MORISE There is only the woman's testimony.

ANDRÉ BRETON Does Unik share this opinion?

PIERRE UNIK I think not in some cases. I think the woman can be aware of it.

BENJAMIN PÉRET When?

PIERRE UNIK When the woman can perceive a change in the man's demeanour.

ANDRÉ BRETON That is entirely subjective and worthless. Is there nothing else?

PIERRE UNIK Why do you think that it is worthless because it is subjective?

ANDRÉ BRETON Because an objective answer can be substituted for that one.

PIERRE UNIK Which one?

ANDRÉ BRETON In most cases the woman can ascertain that the man's orgasm has taken place. She can find out for herself. It is a matter of a more or less conclusive local examination after the man has finished.

BENJAMIN PÉRET That is indeed the only way of telling.

PIERRE UNIK Why do you think that is the only conclusive test for a woman?

ANDRÉ BRETON Because it is the only rational means she can use.

RAYMOND QUENEAU I agree with Breton. She can only tell in this way.

BENJAMIN PÉRET Tanguy?

YVES TANGUY I agree.

ANDRÉ BRETON Prévert?

JACQUES PRÉVERT I agree.

ANDRÉ BRETON Naville?

PIERRE NAVILLE The woman can only tell in this way, and even then she cannot always tell.

ANDRÉ BRETON Why not always?

PIERRE NAVILLE Physiological circumstances sometimes prevent her, due to the very fact of her own orgasm.

ANDRÉ BRETON Is that the only time?

PIERRE NAVILLE I cannot see any others at present.

RAYMOND QUENEAU Explain the phrase 'due to the fact of her own orgasm'.

PIERRE NAVILLE It is self-explanatory.

ANDRÉ BRETON [. . .][2] So Naville believes that, materially, the woman's orgasm and the man's, if they are simultaneous, could be indicated by the emission of seminal fluids which are mixed and indistinguishable?

PIERRE NAVILLE Yes.

BENJAMIN PÉRET Have you yourself noticed such mixing?

PIERRE NAVILLE Obviously, otherwise I wouldn't be talking about it.

ANDRÉ BRETON It is impossible to tell for sure – unless one talks to the woman in a highly questionable way.[3]

PIERRE NAVILLE So what?

BENJAMIN PÉRET Queneau, how do you imagine love between women?

ANDRÉ BRETON Physical love?

BENJAMIN PÉRET Of course.

RAYMOND QUENEAU I imagine that one woman plays the part of the man and the other that of the woman – sixty-nine.

BENJAMIN PÉRET Do you have any direct information on this subject?

RAYMOND QUENEAU No. What I'm saying is drawn from literature and imagination. I have never interviewed a lesbian.

BENJAMIN PÉRET What do you think of homosexuality?

RAYMOND QUENEAU From what point of view? Moral?

BENJAMIN PÉRET If you like.

RAYMOND QUENEAU If two men love each other, I have no moral objections to make to their physical relations.

Protests from Breton, Péret and Unik.[4]

PIERRE UNIK From a physical point of view, I find homosexuality as disgusting as excrement, and from a moral point of view I condemn it.

JACQUES PRÉVERT I agree with Queneau.

RAYMOND QUENEAU It is evident to me that there is an extraordinary prejudice against homosexuality among the surrealists.

ANDRÉ BRETON I accuse homosexuals of confronting human tolerance with a mental and moral deficiency which tends to turn itself into a system and to paralyse every enterprise I respect.[5] I make exceptions though – among them one for the unparalleled case of Sade, and another, more surprising to me, for Lorrain.[6, 7]

PIERRE NAVILLE How do you justify these exceptions?

ANDRÉ BRETON By definition, everything is permitted to a man like the Marquis de Sade, for whom freedom of morals was a matter of life and death. As for Jean Lorrain, I appreciate the remarkable courage he showed in defending what was, for him, a true conviction.

MAX MORISE Why not priests?

ANDRÉ BRETON It is priests who are most opposed to the establishment of this freedom of morals.

BENJAMIN PÉRET What does Tanguy think of homosexuality?

YVES TANGUY I accept it but have no interest in it.

BENJAMIN PÉRET How do you imagine two men making love and what feelings does this arouse in you?

YVES TANGUY I can imagine it in every possible way. I feel total indifference.

PIERRE NAVILLE Prévert, what do you think of onanism?

JACQUES PRÉVERT I don't think anything about it any more. I used to think about it a lot, once, when I practised it.

PIERRE NAVILLE So there is an age at which it would be out of place to practise it?

JACQUES PRÉVERT There is no age as such. It is a matter of individual cases. In itself it is something rather sad.

PIERRE NAVILLE Does it always imply a lack?

JACQUES PRÉVERT For me, yes, always.

YVES TANGUY I think exactly the opposite.

PIERRE NAVILLE Is onanism always accompanied by images of women?

JACQUES PRÉVERT Almost always.

PIERRE NAVILLE What does Breton think of these opinions?

ANDRÉ BRETON They are not mine. Onanism, to the extent that it is acceptable, must be accompanied by images of women. Age does not come into it, there is nothing sad about it, it is a legitimate compensation for some of life's sadnesses.

PIERRE UNIK I completely share that view. But of course onanism can only be a compensation.[8]

RAYMOND QUENEAU I don't believe onanism has anything to do with compensation or consolation. Onanism is as absolutely legitimate in itself as homosexuality.

ANDRÉ BRETON, PIERRE UNIK, BENJAMIN PÉRET They have nothing in common![9]

BENJAMIN PÉRET There cannot be onanism without images of women.

YVES TANGUY How about animals?

ANDRÉ BRETON You're joking!

PIERRE UNIK I share Péret's opinion as regards images of women, but only from puberty.

ANDRÉ BRETON Before and after, as far as I'm concerned.

PIERRE NAVILLE Has Péret had orgasms that were definitely caused by succubi?[10]

BENJAMIN PÉRET Yes.

PIERRE NAVILLE How does such an orgasm compare with those that are obtained in reality?

BENJAMIN PÉRET It is much better.

PIERRE NAVILLE Why?

BENJAMIN PÉRET It is difficult to explain. It is a fact but I cannot explain it. It has only happened two or three times.

PIERRE NAVILLE What distinction do you make between images of women in succubacy[11] and in onanism?

BENJAMIN PÉRET The distinction between dream and waking imagination.

ANDRÉ BRETON That answer couldn't be any vaguer. One difference is that with onanism one chooses what one sees, one is indeed very particular about it, whereas with succubi one does not have a choice.

BENJAMIN PÉRET That's right.

PIERRE NAVILLE With onanism it is always a matter of a woman one knows; with succubi, it is a woman one doesn't know.

YVES TANGUY Is that Morise's opinion of onanism?

MAX MORISE It can be an imaginary woman.

Objections from Naville, Breton, Péret. Approval from Tanguy, Queneau, Prévert.

PIERRE NAVILLE How do you define an imaginary woman?

MAX MORISE A woman who does not resemble any woman you know, but is so to speak made up of different memories.

ANDRÉ BRETON That is merely a matter of changing around real people.

BENJAMIN PÉRET I think it is impossible to produce erotic feeling by imagining a woman.

PIERRE NAVILLE What does Queneau think of the opinions that have been offered regarding succubi?

RAYMOND QUENEAU I share Péret's opinion.

JACQUES PRÉVERT What do you think about mutual masturbation and fellation between two men (non-sodomy)?[12] Would they be homosexuals?

ANDRÉ BRETON Yes. For me, homosexuality is linked to the idea of sodomy. That would be an embryonic form of homosexuality. Does Naville think that one can be the victim of a succubus during passionate love?

PIERRE NAVILLE I think perversity can produce such effects.

RAYMOND QUENEAU One can dream of possessing a woman one knows. What do you think about that?

ANDRÉ BRETON That has nothing whatsoever to do with succubi, and it is an entirely reasonable expression of desire.

BENJAMIN PÉRET What does Prévert think of succubi?

JACQUES PRÉVERT I have only ever dreamt of women I loved.

PIERRE UNIK What does Péret think of female onanism?

BENJAMIN PÉRET I find it just as acceptable as male onanism.

PIERRE UNIK Is that all?

BENJAMIN PÉRET Yes.

PIERRE UNIK And Breton?

ANDRÉ BRETON I have the very highest opinion of it. I am entirely in favour of it.

JACQUES PRÉVERT I agree completely.

PIERRE UNIK Naville?

PIERRE NAVILLE I agree, and I would emphasise that women are much more inclined to it than men.

BENJAMIN PÉRET Have you made any direct observations on this subject?

PIERRE NAVILLE No.

BENJAMIN PÉRET So how can you claim that women are more drawn to it than men?

ANDRÉ BRETON A very fair question.

PIERRE NAVILLE I would make a distinction between verifications and observations.

ANDRÉ BRETON Sophistry.

Approval from Péret and Unik.

BENJAMIN PÉRET Let me then ask you if you have made any verifications?

PIERRE NAVILLE Not really.

BENJAMIN PÉRET So how can you tell?

PIERRE NAVILLE I cannot really.

JACQUES PRÉVERT What is Breton's opinion of sodomy between man and woman?

ANDRÉ BRETON The very highest opinion.[13]

JACQUES PRÉVERT You have already practised it?

ANDRÉ BRETON Indeed.

[. . .] [14]

RAYMOND QUENEAU What does Breton think of physical failures during lovemaking?

ANDRÉ BRETON It can only happen with a woman one loves.

Approval from Péret and Naville.

PIERRE UNIK I think it can happen with any woman.

RAYMOND QUENEAU Do you always make love in the same way? If not, are the variations in order to increase your own pleasure or that of the woman?

ANDRÉ BRETON Very fortunately not, since I would get too bored. As for the woman, she can take the initiative to change as much as she likes.

RAYMOND QUENEAU Péret?

BENJAMIN PÉRET I always follow the woman's preference. I always ask what she prefers.

ANDRÉ BRETON Queneau?

RAYMOND QUENEAU I agree with Péret.

ANDRÉ BRETON Prévert?

JACQUES PRÉVERT I share Breton's view.

ANDRÉ BRETON Morise?

MAX MORISE It is a matter of whatever is mutually agreeable.

BENJAMIN PÉRET Unik?

PIERRE UNIK Like Péret, I always ask the woman what she prefers.

ANDRÉ BRETON I find that absolutely extraordinary, quite phenomenal. Talk about complications!

BENJAMIN PÉRET Tanguy?

YVES TANGUY The same as Morise.

PIERRE UNIK Why does Breton find it extraordinary to ask the woman's opinion?

[. . .] [15]

ANDRÉ BRETON Because it is quite out of place.

PIERRE UNIK It may be the opposite that is out of place.

ANDRÉ BRETON I really don't give a damn. Queneau, in order of preference, which sexual positions do you most enjoy?

RAYMOND QUENEAU Let me see, sodomy, what is known as 'doggy-fashion', sixty-nine. I have no particular feelings for others. I ask Breton the same question.

ANDRÉ BRETON The woman sitting upright astride the man facing him, sixty-nine, sodomy.

PIERRE NAVILLE What role does speech play for you during the sexual act?

ANDRÉ BRETON A greater and greater role as I become more depraved.

RAYMOND QUENEAU What do you mean by depravity?

ANDRÉ BRETON [. . .] [16] Quoting from memory Théodore Jouffroy: 'At twenty I liked blondes; at thirty I prefer brunettes: therefore I am depraved.'

RAYMOND QUENEAU What is Naville's order of preference?

PIERRE NAVILLE I haven't got one.

RAYMOND QUENEAU Péret?

BENJAMIN PÉRET The so-called 'lazy' position, the woman sitting upright with the man lying on his back, sodomy, sixty-nine.[17]

RAYMOND QUENEAU Tanguy?

YVES TANGUY I don't have one.

BENJAMIN PÉRET Morise?

MAX MORISE It changes on different occasions, following a system which is unknown to me.

ANDRÉ BRETON What does Prévert think of the man masturbating in front of the woman and the woman masturbating in front of the man?

JACQUES PRÉVERT I think it's very good.

PIERRE NAVILLE What do you think of mutual masturbation?

JACQUES PRÉVERT It's even better.

ANDRÉ BRETON Is everyone in agreement?

YVES TANGUY No, my preference is for the former.

BENJAMIN PÉRET Mine too.

ANDRÉ BRETON I agree.

MAX MORISE No preference.

BENJAMIN PÉRET What does Tanguy think of male exhibitionism?

YVES TANGUY Uninteresting.

RAYMOND QUENEAU I've never thought about it.

PIERRE UNIK I have the lowest opinion of it.

JACQUES PRÉVERT It leaves me cold.

MAX MORISE I agree. It is of social significance only.

ANDRÉ BRETON It is pathological.

BENJAMIN PÉRET What does Queneau think of female exhibitionism?

RAYMOND QUENEAU It's more interesting than male, because it excites me.

JACQUES PRÉVERT Naville?

PIERRE NAVILLE It can sometimes be desirable.

BENJAMIN PÉRET What do you mean?

PIERRE NAVILLE Perversity, excitement, who knows?

JACQUES PRÉVERT Not only is it desirable, but it seems indispensable (women in public gardens).

PIERRE UNIK I have the lowest opinion of exhibitionism.

BENJAMIN PÉRET Why?

PIERRE UNIK It seems to go against the idea I have of love.

MAX MORISE I have never seen it. It's a sign of hysteria or something like that.

BENJAMIN PÉRET Is that something you would condemn?

MAX MORISE If it's a case of exhibitionism pure and simple, it doesn't interest me, but I think there are always other motivations.

BENJAMIN PÉRET Tanguy?

YVES TANGUY Very desirable.

ANDRÉ BRETON I am against it, but I'm not against semi-exhibitionism.

RAYMOND QUENEAU Has Péret any fetishistic tendencies?

BENJAMIN PÉRET No, not particularly.[18]

RAYMOND QUENEAU Breton?

ANDRÉ BRETON I have an entirely fetishistic conception of love in general. Intellectually, I am strongly inclined to fetishise objects. But in the end I don't practise it at all.

RAYMOND QUENEAU Naville?

PIERRE NAVILLE I have no experience in this field, no specialist knowledge.

ANDRÉ BRETON Does anyone display a taste for a particular object?

No response

ANDRÉ BRETON What does Morise think of physical love between a man and two women?

MAX MORISE It's something I've never done and which does not attract me at all.

ANDRÉ BRETON Unik?

PIERRE UNIK I am rather opposed to it. It doesn't interest me.

ANDRÉ BRETON Péret?

BENJAMIN PÉRET I've tried it, but I was disappointed.[19]

ANDRÉ BRETON Naville?

PIERRE NAVILLE I think it's very desirable. Even more people would be fine.[20]

ANDRÉ BRETON Queneau?

RAYMOND QUENEAU Entirely desirable and commendable.

ANDRÉ BRETON Tanguy?

YVES TANGUY Yes, it's very good.

BENJAMIN PÉRET Breton?

ANDRÉ BRETON Completely against it.

What does Prévert think of brothels?

JACQUES PRÉVERT They don't interest me very much. They could be better. They're useless.

ANDRÉ BRETON Queneau?

RAYMOND QUENEAU They're a fact. They're not very good, but they're better than nothing.

ANDRÉ BRETON Unik?

PIERRE UNIK I have the lowest possible opinion of them.

ANDRÉ BRETON Morise?

MAX MORISE Same answer.

ANDRÉ BRETON Tanguy?

YVES TANGUY A very, very good thing.

ANDRÉ BRETON Naville?

PIERRE NAVILLE It's an institution to be reformed, and the results could be good.

ANDRÉ BRETON Péret?

BENJAMIN PÉRET I have the worst possible opinion of them.

RAYMOND QUENEAU On reflection, I think they're very good.

ANDRÉ BRETON I dream of closing them down.

PIERRE NAVILLE Why?

ANDRÉ BRETON Because they are places where everything has a price, and because they're rather like asylums or prisons.

In what circumstances would Naville consent to sleep with a woman whom he had to pay?

PIERRE NAVILLE In no circumstances. And it has never happened to me.

ANDRÉ BRETON Prévert?

JACQUES PRÉVERT It's never happened to me. *I* have been paid.

ANDRÉ BRETON Unik?

PIERRE UNIK In no circumstances.

ANDRÉ BRETON Queneau?

RAYMOND QUENEAU In circumstances where I find the woman attractive.

ANDRÉ BRETON Morise?

MAX MORISE Under no circumstances.

ANDRÉ BRETON Péret?

BENJAMIN PÉRET It's happened to me, but without my knowing in advance. Each time I was the greenhorn.

ANDRÉ BRETON Tanguy?

YVES TANGUY If I find the woman attractive.

PIERRE UNIK Breton?

ANDRÉ BRETON Under no circumstances.

RAYMOND QUENEAU When you make love, do you require certain specific external conditions to be fulfilled? Which ones?

ANDRÉ BRETON At least negative conditions. Nothing external should distract my attention in any annoying way (the wallpaper in the room, the absence of a blind, or a WC).[21]

BENJAMIN PÉRET Light or dark?

ANDRÉ BRETON It varies according to circumstances. I have a horror of the dark, at least the first time.

RAYMOND QUENEAU Péret?

BENJAMIN PÉRET I definitely prefer daylight. As far as other external conditions go, I have a strong preference for making love in woods or beside water.

RAYMOND QUENEAU Naville?

PIERRE NAVILLE I'm completely indifferent.

RAYMOND QUENEAU Morise?

MAX MORISE A minimum of negative conditions. I don't want to be disturbed; I prefer there to be light.

RAYMOND QUENEAU Unik?

PIERRE UNIK A minimum of peace and quiet; I prefer the light.

JACQUES PRÉVERT Nights are for sleeping, days are for making love. My preference is for anywhere that is not a bedroom.

YVES TANGUY Light. As isolated as possible.

ANDRÉ BRETON What does Unik think of making love in a church?

PIERRE UNIK It doesn't interest me at all.

JACQUES PRÉVERT It doesn't appeal to me because of the bells.

RAYMOND QUENEAU I'll never set foot in a church and I wouldn't do so for that.

YVES TANGUY Quite odious.

MAX MORISE Absolutely intolerable idea.

BENJAMIN PÉRET I think of nothing else and have the greatest desire to do it.

ANDRÉ BRETON I am entirely in agreement with Péret and I would want to include every possible refinement.

BENJAMIN PÉRET While I was there I would like to profane the Hosts and, if possible, leave excrement in the chalice.

RAYMOND QUENEAU Would Péret like to make love with a nun?

BENJAMIN PÉRET No, because I find the nun's habit repulsive.

ANDRÉ BRETON It would definitely appeal to me, particularly if she was beautiful. What does Unik think of *frôleuses*?[22]

PIERRE UNIK *Frôlement* is one of the things that excites me the most.

ANDRÉ BRETON Where does this excitement lead you?

PIERRE UNIK That depends on the *frôleuse*, on whether I like her or not.

ANDRÉ BRETON Tanguy?

YVES TANGUY It doesn't interest me.

ANDRÉ BRETON Queneau?

RAYMOND QUENEAU *Frôlement*? It's exciting, but exasperating.

ANDRÉ BRETON Prévert?

[. . .] [23]

YVES TANGUY It doesn't interest me.

[. . .] [24]

PIERRE NAVILLE I don't have any opinion about it.

BENJAMIN PÉRET I find it wonderful. I'm sorry that I don't meet *frôleuses* more often.

ANDRÉ BRETON Quite so. But in effect there really aren't any, and it is probably the case that women don't know how to do it.

MAX MORISE I couldn't care less.

PIERRE UNIK How far does Breton think he can ask a woman to submit to his physical demands?

ANDRÉ BRETON Not in any way. *A priori*, I have no physical demands.

BENJAMIN PÉRET I agree.

ANDRÉ BRETON Must love necessarily be reciprocal?

PIERRE NAVILLE I do not believe it is absolutely necessary, but love vanishes more rapidly without reciprocity.

PIERRE UNIK There is absolutely no need for love to be reciprocal.

BENJAMIN PÉRET It does not have to be reciprocal.

ANDRÉ BRETON It is necessarily reciprocal. For a long time I thought the opposite but I have recently changed my opinion.

What is your favourite age for a woman?

YVES TANGUY Twenty-five upwards.

PIERRE NAVILLE Eighteen to forty.

RAYMOND QUENEAU Fourteen to fifty.

BENJAMIN PÉRET Twenty to twenty-five.

PIERRE UNIK No preference.

JACQUES PRÉVERT Fourteen.

MAX MORISE Around twenty-five.

ANDRÉ BRETON Twenty-three to thirty.

RAYMOND QUENEAU Can lack of cleanliness or scruffiness in a woman prevent you from loving her?

ANDRÉ BRETON Not at all.

BENJAMIN PÉRET Not in the least.

PIERRE UNIK I don't think so.

[. . .] [25]

JACQUES PRÉVERT Not at all.

YVES TANGUY For me, it's an added attraction.

RAYMOND QUENEAU Does Péret like women who limp?

BENJAMIN PÉRET I find that repugnant, along with all other deformities.

MAX MORISE Does anyone think differently?

RAYMOND QUENEAU It appeals to me a lot.

Bestiality does not interest anyone.

ANDRÉ BRETON Would you find it pleasant or unpleasant to make love with a woman who didn't speak French?

BENJAMIN PÉRET It doesn't make any difference at all.

JACQUES PRÉVERT It's very good.[26]

ANDRÉ BRETON Unbearable. I detest foreign languages.

[. . .] [27]

YVES TANGUY Very pleasant.

RAYMOND QUENEAU What importance do you attach to speech during the sexual act?

BENJAMIN PÉRET A great importance in a negative sense. Certain phrases can entirely prevent me from making love.

RAYMOND QUENEAU Considerable importance. Certain words can intensify pleasure.

YVES TANGUY I share that opinion.

PIERRE NAVILLE It is to be encouraged.

JACQUES PRÉVERT I think quite the opposite.

PIERRE UNIK I don't like being spoken to.

ANDRÉ BRETON To what extent and how often can a man and woman making love reach orgasm simultaneously?

YVES TANGUY Very rarely.

BENJAMIN PÉRET What percentage?

YVES TANGUY 10 per cent.

ANDRÉ BRETON Does this frequency vary according to how accustomed you are to making love with a particular woman?.

YVES TANGUY No.

ANDRÉ BRETON This simultaneity we are discussing, is it desirable?

YVES TANGUY Very.

RAYMOND QUENEAU My answers are the same as Tanguy's.

MAX MORISE 15 per cent. Rarer on the first occasion. Desirable.

PIERRE NAVILLE 50 per cent. It doesn't matter.

JACQUES PRÉVERT 8 per cent. (*Does not answer.*) Harmful.

PIERRE UNIK 12 per cent. Don't know. Desirable.

ANDRÉ BRETON Probably never. Greatly desirable.

BENJAMIN PÉRET A minute percentage. Extremely desirable.

Marcel Duhamel.

*Second Session**

31 JANUARY 1928

Louis Aragon

Jacques Baron

Jacques-A. Boiffard

André Breton

Marcel Duhamel

Marcel Noll

Benjamin Péret

Jacques Prévert

Raymond Queneau

Man Ray

Georges Sadoul

Yves Tanguy

Pierre Unik

* The text of this session, like the first, was published in *La révolution surréaliste*, no. 11 (15 March 1928).

LOUIS ARAGON It is a pity we were all unable to give our responses at the same time to the questions posed the other day. Of course it's not possible to go through all those questions again today in the same order, but the subject is far from exhausted.

ANDRÉ BRETON It would be good to hear the opinion of those who were absent on Thursday on the three or four most important questions.

LOUIS ARAGON What were they?

ANDRÉ BRETON The first one we asked, and then possibly the last two.

LOUIS ARAGON A man and a woman make love. To what extent and how often can they reach orgasm simultaneously? Does the frequency vary according to how accustomed you are to making love with a particular woman? Is this simultaneity desirable? What does Man Ray think?

MAN RAY Not frequently. Always possible. Not desirable.

LOUIS ARAGON But how frequently for you?

MAN RAY 75 per cent.

ANDRÉ BRETON Do you try to achieve this simultaneity by artificial methods?

MAN RAY Why artificial? Natural: through calculation and timing.

ANDRÉ BRETON And without such calculation?

MAN RAY Never. I'd always come before the woman, at least the first time.

LOUIS ARAGON Duhamel?

MARCEL DUHAMEL Very frequently indeed. 85 per cent. Usually by artificial methods. Through timing. Three-quarters of the time; it's through my self-restraint that this simultaneity is achieved.[1] Habit is a very important factor for me. The first time it's highly desirable, but very difficult.[2]

LOUIS ARAGON Boiffard?

JACQUES-A. BOIFFARD Without recourse to artificial methods, I think it happens very rarely.

ANDRÉ BRETON Are you opposed to using such methods?

JACQUES-A. BOIFFARD No, I use them.

ANDRÉ BRETON You use them without hesitation, even in the case of love in the true sense?

LOUIS ARAGON I would point out that the way in which Breton asked the last questions is likely to influence the way the next people answer.

ANDRÉ BRETON What percentage for Boiffard?

JACQUES-A. BOIFFARD 50 per cent. But without using the techniques we've been discussing, simultaneity is very rare, and the figures no longer correspond to anything. It's desirable or undesirable depending on the occasion.[3]

LOUIS ARAGON Sadoul?

GEORGES SADOUL Rare. 10 to 15 per cent. Desirable.

ANDRÉ BRETON Using artificial methods?

GEORGES SADOUL Yes.

BENJAMIN PÉRET And without using them?

GEORGES SADOUL It's impossible to give figures.

ANDRÉ BRETON Noll?

MARCEL NOLL From 10 to 15 per cent when it's a woman one is used to; 2 per cent otherwise. Such simultaneity seems to me desirable.

JACQUES BARON From 15 to 45 per cent. 15 per cent for chance encounters, 25 to 45 per cent with women to whom one has a romantic attachment.

ANDRÉ BRETON Aragon?

LOUIS ARAGON I would put the questions the other way round. This simultaneity is precisely what seems to me to be most desirable in love. It is something absolutely exceptional. Of course, it is completely impossible for me to induce it. I have neither the mental nor the physical capacity to produce such a result. Perhaps that means that it is really a moral issue for me, I don't know, but probably it is. What is certain is that I am completely incapable of delaying my own orgasm. Which makes it impossible to talk about percentages: maybe 1 per cent. I don't think that the fact that I know a woman has any influence in this respect.

It seems important to me to draw some conclusions from all that has just been said. I would like it if someone who was here the other night could ask some supplementary questions.

ANDRÉ BRETON That's quite difficult. For myself, I agree with Aragon, approximately at least: 0 or 1 per cent. I refuse to have recourse to artificial methods when it's a question of love, and it is a moral issue for me.

The alternative would be libertinism.

[. . .][4]

JACQUES-A. BOIFFARD I object to the phrase 'artificial methods'. Whatever you call them, it seems to me that they are less a matter of cold calculation than of mutual understanding.

Approval from Baron and Prévert.

RAYMOND QUENEAU I would like to know what Aragon thinks of homosexuality.

LOUIS ARAGON I will answer that later. One important question is whether a man and a woman can recognise each other's orgasms. Are there effectively ways of knowing? Noll?

MARCEL NOLL No. Neither the man or the woman has any objective means of telling.

LOUIS ARAGON Sadoul?

GEORGES SADOUL There are ways.

LOUIS ARAGON Explain yourself.

GEORGES SADOUL I'm quite unable to express myself on this subject.

[. . .][5]

ANDRÉ BRETON Is it not a material fact that the woman can recognise the man's orgasm? When he ejaculates?

GEORGES SADOUL Yes.

ANDRÉ BRETON At the moment it happens?

GEORGES SADOUL Yes, without any doubt.

ANDRÉ BRETON Does the man have any comparable way of recognising the woman's orgasm?

GEORGES SADOUL No.

ANDRÉ BRETON Man Ray?

MAN RAY The woman is strongly aware of the precise moment of orgasm in the man. But the man has nothing to go on except for the woman's lassitude.

ANDRÉ BRETON And if this lassitude is simulated?

MAN RAY Too bad for the woman. I go along with her act.

ANDRÉ BRETON Given this, it would be wildly optimistic to talk of orgasm being simultaneous in 75 per cent[6] of cases.

MAN RAY If it's simply a matter of physical satisfaction, onanism seems to me to be ideal. Making love with a woman is a game whose object is to arrive at orgasm together.

JACQUES BARON I think that the woman is aware of the man's orgasm at the moment of ejaculation, but I am not absolutely certain.

MARCEL DUHAMEL It can only be a matter either of absolute certainty or of doubt.

JACQUES BARON There are obviously cases when the woman is not aware of the man's orgasm.

LOUIS ARAGON What cases?

JACQUES BARON They are not clearly defined.

ANDRÉ BRETON Can the man fake orgasm?

PIERRE UNIK Obviously, since there are times when the woman is mistaken even without the man faking.

[. . .][7]

LOUIS ARAGON As regards simulated orgasm, there are certainly professionals. Personally, I don't think the woman can ever be absolutely sure that the man has had an orgasm if she is only judging by secondary signs – she can only be sure when by touch or sight she can tell that ejaculation has indeed taken place.

JACQUES-A. BOIFFARD Could it not be said that a man has had an orgasm simply because it is evident that there has been ejaculation?

LOUIS ARAGON For me, ejaculation is accompanied by orgasm.

RAYMOND QUENEAU Not necessarily in my case.

JACQUES PRÉVERT Nor mine.

YVES TANGUY No, not at all.

[. . .][8]

ANDRÉ BRETON These can only be pathological cases.[9]

LOUIS ARAGON I must point out that for the first time during this discussion the word 'pathological' has been brought up. That seems to suggest that some of us believe in the idea of the normal man. I object to this idea.

Protests from Breton, Baron, Duhamel and Péret. Approval from various participants.[10]

ANDRÉ BRETON I would be interested to know what explanation Aragon gives of the phenomenon of non-orgasm.

LOUIS ARAGON I don't have one. I have no experience of it. Moreover, if the man has no material means of recognising the woman's orgasm, he obviously has subjective ones, which could not be the basis of these percentages to which I object. For me, it would be impossible to make love with a woman if I thought that she was pretending.

ANDRÉ BRETON What prevents a man from materially perceiving a woman's orgasm?

MARCEL NOLL I don't know.

JACQUES PRÉVERT A man is the best judge of a man's orgasm; and a woman is the best judge of a woman's orgasm.

ANDRÉ BRETON There is a perfectly material reason preventing him: the impossibility for a man to distinguish between his own emissions and the woman's various emissions, or even between the different emissions of the woman.

PIERRE UNIK So, to conclude, it seems that there are only subjective signs unless the woman makes a local examination.

LOUIS ARAGON Do Boiffard and Duhamel agree?

JACQUES-A. BOIFFARD I don't think there are any objective signs in the majority of cases, but, as Breton said, given the impossibility of distinguishing between the various emissions of the woman (which could only be distinguished with the aid of a microscope), there is no practical way of knowing. As for the opposite question (the objective signs of a man's orgasm), I don't know.

LOUIS ARAGON Duhamel?

MARCEL DUHAMEL I obviously don't think there are any objective signs, but I put no faith in anything except mutual trust. I refuse to consider what could happen without it.

LOUIS ARAGON Like the other day, let us ask: (1) How far can this trust be expected to go? (2) Do you think simulation is legitimate?

MARCEL DUHAMEL (1) It is obviously a result of mutual desire. (2) Absolutely not.

[. . .][11]

JACQUES PRÉVERT (1) I don't think it has any bearing on the matter. (2) I will always believe in the legitimacy of simulation.

ANDRÉ BRETON I have already answered the first question. (2) Sometimes I am not opposed to such simulation.

LOUIS ARAGON Queneau?

RAYMOND QUENEAU I do not trust anyone, especially not a woman; (2) I find all simulation legitimate.

BENJAMIN PÉRET I strongly protest. I will always trust a woman if I love her. I think simulation is legitimate, although I have no desire to practise it.

RAYMOND QUENEAU Even if I love her I don't trust her, especially not in this area.

LOUIS ARAGON For me, the day I stop trusting a woman, I stop loving her. I hate a woman faking, although, ideally, I find it legitimate. For my part, I'd very much like to be able to pretend, but I'm physically incapable.

JACQUES BARON I completely trust a woman whom I love and whom I believe loves me.

GEORGES SADOUL I agree with that statement.

JACQUES BARON I am not against simulation, but it is cheating as far as love is concerned.

PIERRE UNIK I think simulation is legitimate and is not a matter of cheating when the woman does it in order to give the man an orgasm if she desires it.

BENJAMIN PÉRET Does Duhamel acknowledge the possibility of making love with a woman if he loves another?

MARCEL DUHAMEL For me it's very possible.

MARCEL NOLL It is out of the question. When I love a woman I don't look at other women.

RAYMOND QUENEAU I would simply like to ask Péret and Noll what they understand by loving a woman.

MARCEL NOLL I'm saying that I have no interest in making love with a woman when I love another.

RAYMOND QUENEAU What does it mean to love a woman?

BENJAMIN PÉRET I cannot be asked to give a definition like that at the drop of a hat.

MARCEL NOLL Not being in love at the moment, I cannot say what it means to love a woman. I don't trust memories.

ANDRÉ BRETON It is curious to observe that no one here can say what it means to love a woman.[12]

LOUIS ARAGON I can. To love a woman is to see her as the unique preoccupation of one's life, a preoccupation above all others.

BENJAMIN PÉRET Baron, is it possible for you to make love to a woman when you love another?

JACQUES BARON My answer would be the same as Noll's. It wouldn't interest me; I don't *see* other women.

LOUIS ARAGON I am capable of it, but with one restriction, which is simply that this episode takes its place within a wider experience, not so much mine as that of the woman I love (her anger).

JACQUES BARON Noll, what do you think of homosexuality?

MARCEL NOLL I can only talk about homosexuals. I feel nothing but a deep, visceral antipathy to such people. There is no similarity whatsoever between their values and mine.

JACQUES BARON Man Ray?

MAN RAY I don't see any great physical distinction between the love of a man for a woman and homosexuality. It is the emotional ideas of homosexuals which have always separated me from them: emotional relations between men have always seemed to me worse than between men and women.

RAYMOND QUENEAU I find these emotional relations equally acceptable in both cases.

ANDRÉ BRETON Are you a homosexual, Queneau?

RAYMOND QUENEAU No. Can we hear Aragon's view of homosexuality?

LOUIS ARAGON Homosexuality seems to me to be a sexual inclination like any other. I don't see it as a matter for any kind of moral condemnation, and, although I might criticise particular homosexuals for the same reasons I'd criticise 'ladies' men', I don't think this is the place to do so.

JACQUES BARON I share that opinion.

MARCEL DUHAMEL I do not believe that moral viewpoints have any place in this question. I'm generally annoyed by the external affectations and feminine mannerisms of homosexuals. Nonetheless I've been able to imagine without revulsion – for a short space of time – going to bed with some young man whom I found particularly beautiful.

JACQUES-A. BOIFFARD Not all homosexuals indulge in such affectations. The mannerisms of some women are more ridiculous, more annoying, than those of some homosexuals. I absolutely do not condemn homosexuality from a moral point of view. I too have imagined going to bed with a man without any revulsion. Though I haven't done it.

ANDRÉ BRETON I am absolutely opposed to continuing the discussion of this subject. If this promotion of homosexuality carries on, I will leave this meeting forthwith.

LOUIS ARAGON It has never been a question of promoting homosexuality. This discussion is becoming reactive. My own response, which I would like to elaborate upon, isn't to homosexuality so much as to the fact that it has become an issue for us. I want to talk about all sexual inclinations.

ANDRÉ BRETON Do people want me to abandon this discussion? I am quite happy to demonstrate my obscurantism on this subject.

RAYMOND QUENEAU Do you condemn everything that is called sexual perversion, Breton?

ANDRÉ BRETON In no way.

RAYMOND QUENEAU Which perversions don't you condemn?

ANDRÉ BRETON All apart from the one we have been discussing for too long.

RAYMOND QUENEAU What does Aragon think of using condoms?

LOUIS ARAGON I have a childish image of them. I believe you buy them in chemists'.

ANDRÉ BRETON More usually in household stores, I think.[13]

RAYMOND QUENEAU It's odd, I have exactly the same image of them as Aragon.

LOUIS ARAGON Let's continue. Do any of us make use of objects for erotic purposes?

Unanimous no.

LOUIS ARAGON Queneau, is the presence of a third person a hindrance when you are making love?

RAYMOND QUENEAU No.

MARCEL DUHAMEL The presence of a man would greatly disturb me, but not of a woman.

MARCEL NOLL The presence of a man who was also making love might not disturb me, if it was unavoidable.

JACQUES BARON The presence of voyeurs disturbs me, but not that of other active participants.

GEORGES SADOUL I go along with that.

MAN RAY A stranger would disturb me, but not a friend. A woman, never.

JACQUES-A. BOIFFARD My answer is the same as Baron's.

PIERRE UNIK The presence of a third person in any circumstances would disturb me and prevent me from making love.

JACQUES PRÉVERT It's quite disturbing.

ANDRÉ BRETON I could not bear the presence of any third person.

LOUIS ARAGON Love is made by two people, in different kinds of solitude. It can be in a crowd, but an oblivious crowd.

BENJAMIN PÉRET The presence of a woman does not bother me but any other presence is intolerable.

ANDRÉ BRETON What sexual positions do you enjoy most? Baron?

JACQUES BARON Sixty-nine, so-called 'doggy-fashion'.

MARCEL DUHAMEL So-called 'doggy-fashion', sixty-nine.

LOUIS ARAGON I'm very limited. The various positions all attract me equally, as so many impossibilities. What I enjoy most is coming when I am performing cunnilingus. In the end I almost always make love in the simplest way.

MAN RAY No preferences. What intrigues me most is fellation of the man by the woman, because that's the thing that has happened to me most rarely.

MARCEL NOLL Cunnilingus, or sex on sex, mouth on mouth, sixty-nine.

GEORGES SADOUL No strong preference. Cunnilingus, I suppose.

LOUIS ARAGON What excites you most?

MARCEL DUHAMEL A woman's legs and thighs. And then the sex, the thighs [sic] and the buttocks.

JACQUES PRÉVERT Buttocks.

RAYMOND QUENEAU The arse.

LOUIS ARAGON The thought of the woman's orgasm.

MARCEL NOLL That's the only thing that interests me, too.

MARCEL DUHAMEL Me too.

MARCEL PÉRET As regards parts of the body, the legs and breasts. Beyond that, seeing a woman masturbating.

MAN RAY The breasts and armpits.

ANDRÉ BRETON The eyes and breasts. Apart from that, everything in physical love which pertains to perversity.

LOUIS ARAGON I would endorse the second part of that answer in so far as perversity is waste.

ANDRÉ BRETON For me it is not necessarily sterile pleasure.

JACQUES BARON The mouth, the teeth, the base of the breasts. Everything to do with perversity and experiment.

GEORGES SADOUL The sex and the top of the thighs, then the mouth. Everything to do with perversity and experiment.

PIERRE UNIK The image I have of the excitement of the woman I love.

LOUIS ARAGON What do you think about external danger (mortal danger, for example) when you are making love?

JACQUES PRÉVERT It can only be a stimulant, and people who have never known such a danger have never made love.

ANDRÉ BRETON I find that remark entirely excessive. There's no question of being aware of external danger during physical love with a woman you love.

MARCEL DUHAMEL I might be aware of such danger when I'm making love with a woman I love. It would not be a stimulant but – and I find it hard to explain – it would give me a more powerful orgasm, as long as the danger wasn't immediate and catastrophic.

MARCEL NOLL The idea of such danger has never crossed my mind.

LOUIS ARAGON I used to have a great taste for danger until the day when it appeared in the form off a threat which particularly affected the woman I loved. Since then I have dreaded it.

ANDRÉ BRETON Was it a mortal danger?

LOUIS ARAGON For that woman, no.

GEORGES SADOUL Without doubt I find the idea of danger a stimulant.

RAYMOND QUENEAU When I'm making love I'm too preoccupied to think about danger.

BENJAMIN PÉRET I absolutely agree with that.

LOUIS ARAGON In my case, any little thing can distract me.

RAYMOND QUENEAU That's also true.

ANDRÉ BRETON Love is perhaps compatible with all kinds of distractions, but the idea of love cannot endure any.

LOUIS ARAGON Quite so.

RAYMOND QUENEAU Does Aragon have any fetishistic tendencies?

LOUIS ARAGON I take myself to be a fetishist in the sense that I always carry a large number of objects which are important to me and which must always be within reach.

MARCEL DUHAMEL I'm like Aragon.

ANDRÉ BRETON To what extent does Aragon think an erection is necessary in the accomplishment of the sexual act?

LOUIS ARAGON Some degree of erection is necessary, but in my case I've never had anything but semi-erections.

ANDRÉ BRETON Do you regret that?

LOUIS ARAGON As much as any other physical failure, and no more. I don't regret it any more than being unable to lift pianos.

MARCEL DUHAMEL Does Aragon attach more importance to the man's orgasm than the woman's?

LOUIS ARAGON It depends on the occasion.

Before leaving, I must declare that what disturbs me about the majority of answers given here is the notion which I believe I detect of the inequality of the man and the woman. For myself, nothing can be said about physical love if one doesn't start from the fact that men and women have equal rights in it.

ANDRÉ BRETON Who has claimed the contrary?

LOUIS ARAGON Let me explain: the validity of all that has been said so far seems to me to have been partially undermined by the inevitable predominance of the male point of view.

RAYMOND QUENEAU What is Noll's opinion of fetishism?

MARCEL NOLL I'm very much a fetishist: I keep all kinds of objects at home.

ANDRÉ BRETON That isn't fetishism, it's a mania for collecting.

MARCEL NOLL I don't masturbate using objects belonging to women.

GEORGES SADOUL Until now I've never given the least thought to fetishism or collection-manias.

MARCEL DUHAMEL I have fetishistic tendencies.

ANDRÉ BRETON Is Queneau a masochist, in the widest sense of the word?

RAYMOND QUENEAU Not at all. I'm more of a sadist.

GEORGES SADOUL I have a strong mental tendency toward masochism and sadism, and I don't necessarily rule them out physically.

MARCEL DUHAMEL Rather sadistic in both senses.

JACQUES BARON [. . .] [14] Rather sadistic in the physical sense.

MARCEL DUHAMEL What importance do you attach to habit in the development of perversions?

ANDRÉ BRETON I'm neither a sadist not a masochist. So habit cannot play any role for me.

MARCEL DUHAMEL Queneau?

RAYMOND QUENEAU As great an importance as in the non-development of perversions.

ANDRÉ BRETON A woman whom, *a priori*, you can love gives herself to you as soon as you desire her. Will you love her more or less than a woman who leaves your desire unfulfilled for a long time?

MARCEL DUHAMEL I will love her much more in the former case.

JACQUES BARON Me too, for I cannot bear coquetry.

BENJAMIN PÉRET I will love her much more in the latter case.

MARCEL NOLL I don't think love can be graduated according to whether you possess the woman sooner or later.

MAN RAY If it's coquetry, less; if it's because of other considerations, more.

RAYMOND QUENEAU More in the former case.

PIERRE UNIK I share Noll's opinion.

JACQUES PRÉVERT It doesn't interest me.

GEORGES SADOUL I undoubtedly love a woman more who is slow to love me than a woman who answers my love at a point where it is not yet close to its greatest intensity.

MARCEL NOLL Immediate possession seems to me to be perfection in this area and, all things considered, the guarantee of love's quality.

ANDRÉ BRETON Infinitely more in the first case, as long as I am sure that she loves me at the moment she gives herself to me.

What is Prévert's opinion of women playing the temptress when it is not certain that love is at stake?

JACQUES PRÉVERT I think it's absolutely fine, and only too rare, which is the fault of men.

MAN RAY I greatly distrust it. I become hostile straight away.

JACQUES PRÉVERT What do you understand by libertinism, Breton?

ANDRÉ BRETON A taste for pleasure for its own sake.

RAYMOND QUENEAU Do you approve or disapprove of it?

ANDRÉ BRETON I categorically disapprove.[15]

PIERRE UNIK Do you think that when a man is a libertine he loses all possibility of loving?

ANDRÉ BRETON Without any doubt.

MARCEL NOLL I think so too.

MAN RAY Can Breton be interested in two women at the same time?

ANDRÉ BRETON I've already said that it is impossible.

And Man Ray?

MAN RAY Yes, but not more than two.

RAYMOND QUENEAU What is your first sexual memory?

BENJAMIN PÉRET At school, when I was seven or eight, I saw a little boy cover his sex with ink and masturbate under the desk.

ANDRÉ BRETON Also at school. A child displaying his sex and referring to it by a word then unknown to me: 'my . . . '[16] That same evening I told the story to my parents.

MARCEL DUHAMEL Still at school. A little boy suddenly putting my hand on his flies. It left me with a very pleasant memory.

JACQUES BARON Pupils masturbating under their portfolios.

MARCEL DUHAMEL I also recall the powerful emotional effect of seeing a man and woman kissing.

MAN RAY I'd passed puberty. An older friend, who must have been sixteen, told me how people made love. I was curious to try it and persuaded a little girl of ten to help by promising to give her a picture book if she would show me her sex. I then tried to penetrate her; she complained that I was hurting her. Afraid of being on my own I had brought along my brother, who was nine, and I persuaded him to try. He succeeded and she clasped him in her arms, saying to me: 'I like your brother better, he doesn't hurt me so much.'

GEORGES SADOUL I have two memories, both from between the age of five and seven, though I don't know which came first. I dreamt I was touching my erect penis and that I broke it off so that it was completely detached from my body, though still erect. I felt absolutely no pain, but was very afraid of the scolding I was sure to receive from my mother the next day. On waking I was greatly relieved to discover that it hadn't happened. And I think I told my mother of my relief.

I also remember caressing a little girl two years younger than me and being caressed by her. These acts were accompanied by smacks on the bottom. We did this at lengthy intervals until I was twelve. The pretext was either that we were playing doctors and nurses or teachers and pupils, taking turns with the roles.

PIERRE UNIK When I was four I dreamt I was in a garden with little girls dressed in white, one of whom was especially beautiful. I stayed with her a long time. I felt a great contentment; when I awoke I was disappointed, and I asked my sister if she had yet had dreams of love.

General protests: 'That's a very feeble sexual memory.'

PIERRE UNIK I have others. Around five or six I imagined that I was clasping an animal in my arms, sometimes a horse, sometimes a dog.

I felt an indefinable sensation. I felt the same sensation watching dogs together in the street, which I thought were playing. And I felt it too when reading a story entitled 'Flesh' in a book translated from Russian and published by Ferenczi.

JACQUES PRÉVERT My earliest sexual memories concern children of my own age who were interested in nothing but their sexual organs. I was the same. At the age of seven I was shocked by a little girl, the sister of one of my friends, who had fallen over backwards. I could see that she didn't have a sex like me. I concluded that she was disabled. I could no longer bear to see her. She disgusted me. Later she went blind.

RAYMOND QUENEAU I recall getting an erection watching dogs coupling. I also had an orgasm watching a dancer dressed as a page in a revue at the Folies-Bergère. There were two dancers on stage; I was only interested in the one on the left.

MARCEL NOLL I must have been four or four and a half. A boy with whom I usually walked home one day invited me in to meet his mother. He told her in front of me that he wished that his little blue tweed trousers were tighter. I only know that, deeply affected by this episode, I described it to my parents that same evening. They looked at each other for a long time; I blushed and felt deeply embarrassed. That embarrassment lasted for a good while.

Max Morise. Photograph by Jacques-André Boiffard.

Third Session

BETWEEN 1 AND 14 FEBRUARY 1928

Louis Aragon

André Breton

Max Morise

Marcel Noll

Benjamin Péret

BENJAMIN PÉRET Noll, you told us last time about your earliest sexual memories. Was a feeling of shame in any way attached to those memories?

MARCEL NOLL Oh yes, for sure.

BENJAMIN PÉRET And in what way?

MARCEL NOLL I think that in a conscious sense my shame was born out of observing the reaction I had provoked in my parents when I told them the story you heard.

BENJAMIN PÉRET Perhaps Morise, who did not contribute last time, could now tell us one of his earliest sexual memories?

MAX MORISE The earliest sexual memory I can recall at present is the impression made on me by the penis of a horse, harnessed to a coal-wagon parked outside the yard of Armes de France in the avenue de Breteuil. No feeling of shame whatsoever is attached to this memory.

BENJAMIN PÉRET Aragon?

LOUIS ARAGON I was a slow developer where shame's concerned and it is an emotion which is still not fully developed.

ANDRÉ BRETON I protest at the flippant nature of that answer.

BENJAMIN PÉRET At what point did you feel the first stirrings of shame?

LOUIS ARAGON I've forgotten, probably out of shame.

BENJAMIN PÉRET What is your first conscious memory of feeling shame?

LOUIS ARAGON I cannot call any memory the first because something in me rebels against this subject, by definition.

BENJAMIN PÉRET I don't understand. That seems rather strange to me.

LOUIS ARAGON To gratify Péret I will answer that my first conscious feeling of shame coincided with the first time when it could be said that I was in love.

BENJAMIN PÉRET Breton?

ANDRÉ BRETON The awakening of shame in me does not seem to coincide with my first sexual memory, which I have already recounted to you. It must be slightly later and is linked to the feeling of rebellion I experienced when, at around the age of six, my mother took me to the doctor to ask his advice on five or six episodes of bedwetting. The doctor asked my mother if I had any 'bad habits'. In the most vulgar sense of the phrase, I did not.

LOUIS ARAGON I would like to know, Péret, if for each person here, sexual shame was the first kind they experienced?

BENJAMIN PÉRET For me, yes.

MARCEL NOLL For me, no.

BENJAMIN PÉRET A short time after the events I described, perhaps a year later, the concierge found me masturbating under a staircase to the courtyard of my parents' house. After that I no longer dared go down into the courtyard.

LOUIS ARAGON Before that you hadn't felt any stirring of shame, for whatever reason?

BENJAMIN PÉRET I have no memory of one.

Noll?

MARCEL NOLL I do have a memory, predating the first memory I told you about, which seems to me to reveal a shame having nothing to do with sex.

BENJAMIN PÉRET Aragon?

LOUIS ARAGON For a very long time, shame for me was a social feeling directed against my family (the notion that it was inferior). Later I became conscious of it when I read books in which little boys and girls had bad feeling towards their parents.

ANDRÉ BRETON This has nothing to do with shame. It is obvious that shame cannot be anything but sexual.

LOUIS ARAGON Quite probably the social form of shame in me is nothing but a disguised form of sexual shame.

ANDRÉ BRETON One might wish for people to have rather more self-awareness and perceive the basic form of shame underlying these so-called social forms.

LOUIS ARAGON A wish which is entirely idealistic.

ANDRÉ BRETON Nevertheless, the question is far from settled. If in a discussion of shame one can claim that by definition it is impossible to overcome one's own shame, there is no way of continuing.

LOUIS ARAGON What a shame you're so inhibited!

ANDRÉ BRETON What wit!

LOUIS ARAGON What is wit?

BENJAMIN PÉRET Third-rate humour.

ANDRÉ BRETON And systematic obstruction.

Aragon, what is shame?

LOUIS ARAGON A question which I am incapable of answering.

ANDRÉ BRETON Then I ask Péret, who is certainly capable of answering.

BENJAMIN PÉRET It's a feeling of embarrassment which I have felt and now feel less and less, for example in being seen naked. I have a certain shame about showing myself naked in front of men, but far less in front of women.

ANDRÉ BRETON Morise?

MAX MORISE I'll tell you a little story that's been told to me about when I was a child. One day, after I'd had a bath, a maid came into my room at a moment when I had my back to the door. I quickly turned round covering my bottom with a towel.

MARCEL NOLL Shame is a feeling which has to be mastered. In my case it was born out of others' incomprehension of some of my actions, an incomprehension to which I attached too much importance. I felt I wasn't as good as other people.

ANDRÉ BRETON To take up Noll's felicitous phrase, shame is a feeling which should *not* be mastered. It is a feeling of absurd embarrassment about something, which as we know can be sublimated, but hardly excused because of that. It is never incomprehensible and can always be traced back to a basic pattern of a sexual nature, which can be overcome. There is no justification for it, merely an excuse: it is provoked by a sadness a man feels when he has to contemplate the supposed existence of his body – in other words, it is a Christian sentiment.

LOUIS ARAGON Very good.

BENJAMIN PÉRET For my part, I'd make some distinction between purely sexual shame and its emotional variations.

What does Noll think?

MARCEL NOLL I wouldn't make any distinction.

LOUIS ARAGON It's hard to answer now because the earliest questions were more concerned with shame's origins than its essence. But now – and not before time – let's move on to adult life. And here I would hope that non-emotional shame no longer exists. Emotional shame is precisely what I've said I find difficult to discuss.

ANDRÉ BRETON I do not conceive of any break between childhood and adult life. And I still deny emotional shame: as Péret said, the essential thing is to know whether or not one can allow oneself to be seen naked.

BENJAMIN PÉRET I'm not embarrassed to be seen naked, but I can find it difficult to talk about an emotional adventure.

ANDRÉ BRETON I no longer understand.

LOUIS ARAGON If it's really a matter of whether or not one can allow oneself to be seen naked, then I have no shame.

ANDRÉ BRETON Would Aragon have no objection to appearing before a woman wearing only socks and suspenders?

LOUIS ARAGON As soon as I'm asked the question, I want to answer no, because I can picture myself in such apparel. But it could happen. My shame here isn't related to the woman but to André Breton.

ANDRÉ BRETON The first part of that answer is highly ambiguous. Isn't Aragon aware of what he's wearing when he's naked?

LOUIS ARAGON Not always.

[. . .][1]

BENJAMIN PÉRET Would anyone allow themselves to be seen by a woman with suspicious stains on his trousers?

MAX MORISE I'm not in the habit of going along the street with suspicious stains.

BENJAMIN PÉRET Noll?

MARCEL NOLL No more than I would with my flies undone.

BENJAMIN PÉRET Aragon?

LOUIS ARAGON I don't see how there could be any suspicious stains on my trousers.

BENJAMIN PÉRET Breton?

ANDRÉ BRETON Under no circumstances would I enter the presence of a woman who was likely to find suspicious stains on my trousers.

LOUIS ARAGON Perfect.

ANDRÉ BRETON What does Noll think of the idea of waiting naked in bed for a woman to undress?

MARCEL NOLL I don't like the idea at all. But it's not impossible that such a thing should happen.

ANDRÉ BRETON Aragon?

LOUIS ARAGON There's a distinction to be made. Are we talking about a woman who doesn't know you, or a woman who knows you well. In the first case, it's outrageous, in the second, purely a matter of chance.

And you?

ANDRÉ BRETON [. . .] [2] Rather curious.

Péret, you go into a bedroom with a woman. Do you start to undress first?

BENJAMIN PÉRET No, not usually.

ANDRÉ BRETON Why?

BENJAMIN PÉRET Because it's seeing the woman beginning to undress which encourages me to do the same.

ANDRÉ BRETON Do you wait for the woman to be ready before you get into bed?

BENJAMIN PÉRET No, I don't wait.

ANDRÉ BRETON Noll, same question.

MARCEL NOLL It depends entirely on the woman in question. Until now, no.

ANDRÉ BRETON Why until now?

MARCEL NOLL How would I know?

ANDRÉ BRETON Aragon, same question.

LOUIS ARAGON If it's a woman I don't know at all . . .

ANDRÉ BRETON Of course.

LOUIS ARAGON No, I don't undress first. Because that's not how my desire works. (1) I'm thinking of undressing her rather than undressing myself. (2) The woman's undressing may take some time, whereas it takes me no time at all.

ANDRÉ BRETON Do you wait for her to be ready before getting into bed?

LOUIS ARAGON In such circumstances, I don't get into bed. We go to bed together.

ANDRÉ BRETON Morise, same question.

MAX MORISE I think not.

ANDRÉ BRETON Why?

MAX MORISE (*Long silence.*)

LOUIS ARAGON Same question .

ANDRÉ BRETON (1) No, at least to the question of waiting in bed for a woman. (2) Because I don't want to give the impression that I'm in a hurry when I'm not. (3) No, I don't wait for her to be ready.

BENJAMIN PÉRET Morise, do you wash in front of a woman after making love?

ANDRÉ BRETON And does Noll always wash after making love?

MAX MORISE (1) No.

MARCEL NOLL (2) No, not always.

ANDRÉ BRETON Why sometimes?

MARCEL NOLL Because the times when I haven't washed are when I forget. I have other preoccupations.

ANDRÉ BRETON I wonder what they might be.

LOUIS ARAGON I wash when I'm dirty. A woman cannot make me dirty. At the most, I might give myself a wipe.

ANDRÉ BRETON But it's you who may make yourself dirty.

LOUIS ARAGON That happens so rarely.

BENJAMIN PÉRET I always wash after making love. The only times I haven't are when the woman has insisted that I stay by her.

ANDRÉ BRETON I always wash, except after sixty-nine.

BENJAMIN PÉRET Of course.

ANDRÉ BRETON Does Aragon enjoy seeing a woman wash herself before making love with her.

LOUIS ARAGON I see no objection to it. It doesn't interest me in the slightest. In some cases, I could find it appealing, but that would be because of the woman's posture, not because of what she was doing.

ANDRÉ BRETON Morise?

MAX MORISE No.

ANDRÉ BRETON Noll?

MARCEL NOLL Absolutely not. I can't bear all the paraphernalia of washing.

ANDRÉ BRETON Péret?

BENJAMIN PÉRET It doesn't appeal to me.

MARCEL NOLL Breton?

ANDRÉ BRETON I have an absolutely passionate interest in it.

What does Noll think about the hero of one of Boccaccio's stories, who fell asleep while the woman he'd just made love with was holding his sex? Could he do that?

MARCEL NOLL Certainly.

ANDRÉ BRETON Aragon?

LOUIS ARAGON As M. Paul Valéry said, one can go to sleep on any idea.

ANDRÉ BRETON Morise?
MAX MORISE That strikes me as true.
ANDRÉ BRETON Péret?
BENJAMIN PÉRET I don't see how it would be possible to sleep in such circumstances.
ANDRÉ BRETON Very good. Exactly. Does Morise let a woman touch his sex when it's not erect?
MAX MORISE Why not?
ANDRÉ BRETON Péret?
BENJAMIN PÉRET In no circumstances. I would feel diminished.
ANDRÉ BRETON That's exactly the right word.
Noll?
MARCEL NOLL I hate it.[3]
ANDRÉ BRETON Aragon?
LOUIS ARAGON If a woman touched my sex only when it was erect, it wouldn't get that way very often.
BENJAMIN PÉRET Morise, you imagine a women in the most extreme or degrading physical positions, like those described by Huysmans. What influence do these images have on your desire for that woman?
MAX MORISE I don't nurture such images.
LOUIS ARAGON I don't have degrading images of a woman I love.
MARCEL NOLL I don't nurture such images. Even if they came to me, they would have no influence.
BENJAMIN PÉRET How can you know since it's never happened to you?
MARCEL NOLL I suppose because of the idea I have of love.
ANDRÉ BRETON In passionate love understood in its most violent form, these physical images must be very powerful.
BENJAMIN PÉRET When it's a woman I love, no position can disgust me. All are pleasing.
LOUIS ARAGON Péret, are you ashamed of your own pleasure?
BENJAMIN PÉRET In no way.
LOUIS ARAGON Do you find the external manifestations of that pleasure (shouts, moans, curses) to be something desirable?
BENJAMIN PÉRET That happens extremely rarely, but I'm not embarrassed by it. (In all, perhaps ten times.)
LOUIS ARAGON Noll?
MARCEL NOLL (1) No. (2) The shouts and other manifestations are provoked by desire itself and I'm not ashamed of it.

LOUIS ARAGON Do you shout?

MARCEL NOLL I have done.

BENJAMIN PÉRET I would like to know in what circumstances.

MARCEL NOLL When I've come and I'm angry that I came at that particular moment and so I curse the fact that I've come. Those are the only times I've cried out up till now.

LOUIS ARAGON Morise?

MAX MORISE (1) No shame. (2) I would love to cry out . . .

LOUIS ARAGON Breton?

ANDRÉ BRETON (1) No, because I don't know pleasure.

BENJAMIN PÉRET By pleasure I mean orgasm.

ANDRÉ BRETON I'm happy to carry on playing with words as long as you want. (2) Shouts, external manifestations, pretence, yes, in the sense of simulation, of course.

BENJAMIN PÉRET Aragon?

LOUIS ARAGON (1) No, because I am very proud of my pleasure. (2) Despite myself, I sometimes say, 'Nom de Dieu!'

[. . .][4]

ANDRÉ BRETON Aragon, you've made love, you think you're ready to begin again, you try. You are tired. What happens to you?

LOUIS ARAGON I become very unhappy.

ANDRÉ BRETON What do you do?

LOUIS ARAGON I apologise, often very awkwardly.

ANDRÉ BRETON Péret?

BENJAMIN PÉRET I never try to make love again unless I'm sure I can do it.

ANDRÉ BRETON How can you be sure?

BENJAMIN PÉRET Through a kind of intuition.

[. . .][5]

ANDRÉ BRETON Noll?

MARCEL NOLL I have no experience of it, because of the way I make love. The first time, I delay my own orgasm as long as possible. Then I can make love a second time. A third or fourth time – out of the question.

ANDRÉ BRETON Morise?

MAX MORISE It has happened to me. It's a very unpleasant feeling.

ANDRÉ BRETON Inexpressible anguish. I make whatever excuse I can and await with despair the moment when I am sure I can start again.

This is one of the things which has given rise in me to the idea of time in its full horror. It is also one of several points of entry for the notion of simulation in physical love.[6]

What does Aragon think of the sexual temperament of a woman?

LOUIS ARAGON In a general sense, the woman's sexual temperament seems to me to be the origin of many strange and interesting things, but in a personal sense I am grateful to a woman who hides it from me, something which I think all those women who appeared to me to have a mild temperament were in fact doing.

ANDRÉ BRETON Noll?

MARCEL NOLL I'm excessively sensitive to the sexual temperament of women. It has always seemed to me to be an effect whose cause I don't know. A woman's sexual appetite spurs me on enormously. I am deeply affected by it.

ANDRÉ BRETON Morise?

MAX MORISE Too strong a sexual temperament in a woman is something I find terribly annoying.

ANDRÉ BRETON Péret?

BENJAMIN PÉRET I very much like women who have plenty of sensuality. Mine increases in proportion to theirs.

ANDRÉ BRETON I see both an absence and an excess of sensuality as very dangerous things. Having to consider the question of a woman's sexual temperament would in itself make me unable to continue to love her.

LOUIS ARAGON In respect of his capacity to make love, how important to Péret is the idea that a woman has of him physically?

BENJAMIN PÉRET Extremely important. If a woman thinks I lack sensuality, then I will lack it.

MARCEL NOLL I never imagine what idea a woman may have of my physical capacities.

LOUIS ARAGON Breton?

ANDRÉ BRETON Perish the woman who would judge me in that way!

LOUIS ARAGON Morise?

MAX MORISE I'd say the same.

BENJAMIN PÉRET Aragon?

LOUIS ARAGON An already very precarious success is at the mercy of the first absurd thought to enter my head. The woman is not responsible for it.

ANDRÉ BRETON A fanciful question: Péret finds all the women with whom he has had sexual relations assembled together, in a café for example, with the one he loved or believed he loved standing apart. What would he do?

BENJAMIN PÉRET Run for my life.

ANDRÉ BRETON Aragon?

LOUIS ARAGON I hope I'd find the necessary presence of mind to take the one I loved out of that dreadful place.

ANDRÉ BRETON Noll?

MARCEL NOLL It could only happen in a nightmare. I would get out of the café along with one of these people, not necessarily the one I had loved.

LOUIS ARAGON Breton?

ANDRÉ BRETON I think I would deliver a grand speech. Its conclusion would be . . . [7]

LOUIS ARAGON Breton, what do you think of modesty in women?

ANDRÉ BRETON I have a very low opinion of it. I see no excuse as long as the woman is beautiful.

LOUIS ARAGON Péret?

BENJAMIN PÉRET It really wears me out. It's completely debilitating.

ANDRÉ BRETON Morise?

MAX MORISE It seems to me both important and appealing. It's something whose absence would change the whole relationship.

MARCEL NOLL I find shame quite incompatible with the idea I have of women.

ANDRÉ BRETON Aragon?

LOUIS ARAGON I have a horror of virgins. I have only had relations with real women who know what love is and make no bones about it.

ANDRÉ BRETON I would like Péret to describe an imaginary woman whom he would find particularly tempting. Eyes, hair, breasts, height, bottom, legs.

BENJAMIN PÉRET Eyes, apple-green and very large, hair black with blue highlights. Breasts, small, far apart, high. Height, from 5′ 5″ to 5′ 6″. Plump bottom. Slender legs, calves right in the middle of the legs.

ANDRÉ BRETON Distinguishing feature?

BENJAMIN PÉRET The same as one I have in my groin: a coffee-coloured mole.

ANDRÉ BRETON Noll?

MARCEL NOLL Dark eyes, very long eyelashes, rather fine eyebrows, black hair, breasts far apart, height, 5′ 4½″, youthful bottom, quite long legs, distinguishing feature: nil.

ANDRÉ BRETON Aragon?

LOUIS ARAGON The woman who would tempt me would not tempt me by her eyes, hair, breasts, height, bottom or legs, but rather by her expression, which is absolutely indescribable.

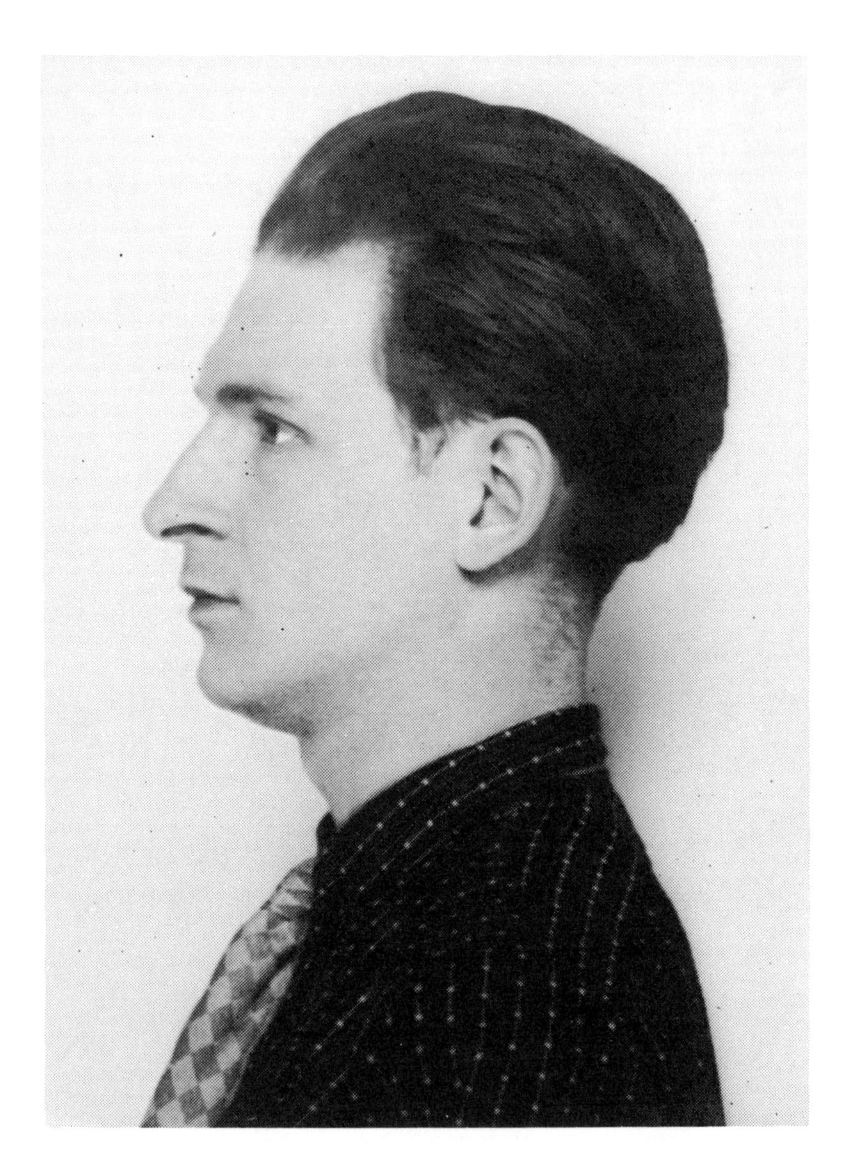

Pierre Naville, 1924.

Fourth Session

15 FEBRUARY 1928

André Breton

Marcel Duhamel

Jean Genbach[1]

Max Morise

Pierre Naville

Jacques Prévert

Yves Tanguy

Pierre Unik

JEAN GENBACH I am astounded by the fact that you are concerned with the sexual question on a physical level, that you can separate it from love.

ANDRÉ BRETON There has never been any question of making such a separation.

JEAN GENBACH I only live to find one woman. I don't give a damn about the rest, nothing exists apart from this woman. I've told you that sexuality doesn't exist, there is only love. That ought to make you tremble with fear, to overwhelm you.

ANDRÉ BRETON Very amusing. Now let us try to be serious. I am not overwhelmed by the question of sex. I dominate it in the name of love.

JEAN GENBACH Love is something you experience in your guts and your brain.

MAX MORISE What do you mean by guts as distinct from brain?

JEAN GENBACH I mean all the fibres of my nerves, all of myself, all that is understood by the word soul.

ANDRÉ BRETON The soul does not exist.

JEAN GENBACH But I claim the soul does exist and that is why I don't agree with you. The idea of the soul is more familiar, more normal to me than the idea of the mind.

MAX MORISE By soul, do you mean that which is distinct from the body?

JEAN GENBACH No. You mean dualism?

ANDRÉ BRETON What is the soul?

JEAN GENBACH I am not sure if that question can be asked.

MAX MORISE Let me be more precise. In what way is the notion of soul superior to the notion of mind and body, or mind?

JEAN GENBACH Because I gain understanding through the mind, whilst the soul is a physical, psychic, emotional, complete part of myself, which most often confronts me with all that is mysterious and unknowable. Merely understanding gives me no great satisfaction.

ANDRÉ BRETON It has never been a question here of mind or soul, of understanding for understanding's sake, or emotion for emotion's sake – we have been discussing life.

JEAN GENBACH If it's a matter of living and talking concretely, I am possessed, and happy to be possessed, by amorous desire. I am not in control of myself, I am not in possession of myself. I don't see what basis there could be for a system which claims that to possess is better than to be possessed.

ANDRÉ BRETON These metaphysical considerations don't interest me and I'd like to move this discussion on.

JEAN GENBACH Then I'd prefer simply to answer your questions.

ANDRÉ BRETON I would like to state that it is unacceptable for Genbach to drag this discussion into an area which has nothing to do with it. I imagine we all have the greatest consideration for his personal background, but the question of possession or domination – of what? – is only being posed here in the most purely formal way and I attach no significance to it. That being so, I would like to ask Genbach what he thinks of homosexuality.

JEAN GENBACH I think it's very good if there is passionate and irresistible love. I do not believe one can oppose one sex to the other.

ANDRÉ BRETON And what of the possibility of a man and woman having simultaneous orgasms?

JEAN GENBACH Until now I have always thought that when I embrace a woman she reaches orgasm when I want her to.

ANDRÉ BRETON Delusions of grandeur. Since Genbach does not oppose mind and body, I'd like to know if he opposes the body to the soul.

JEAN GENBACH Never, I make use of the language we have, but I don't believe there is much of a distinction. What others call my body is my soul.

MAX MORISE What has love got to do with God for you?

JEAN GENBACH I don't know if that means anything. Because I can only answer that I am God and that I deify all that I touch. I cannot create any oppositions within that. There is unity.

PIERRE NAVILLE Is it desirable that priests should be celibate?

JEAN GENBACH I don't give a damn about that. If it's an empirical question, I have the same idea as most people about what goes on. Besides, there are no priests. There is an amorous radiance in everything.

ANDRÉ BRETON Pantheism.

JEAN GENBACH It is precisely the panpsychism that you attribute to everything which astonishes me.

ANDRÉ BRETON There is no trace of any such thing.

PIERRE NAVILLE Can a practising priest love a woman?

JEAN GENBACH Certainly. It is difficult for me to see any obstacles for the good reason that I have always been in revolt, for the last five, six years.

ANDRÉ BRETON You are not accepting the rules of this game.

JEAN GENBACH I've told you what I think of this discussion.

ANDRÉ BRETON So don't take part in it. In my opinion your obstructiveness is a function of the complexes which we can perceive in you, purely and simply. It is not a matter of philosophical debate.

MARCEL DUHAMEL You have said that you deny sexuality.

JEAN GENBACH In opposition to love. I can only see one reason for living: to love and to desire.

MARCEL DUHAMEL Yet you refuse to discuss these subjects, love and desire.

JEAN GENBACH Ask me concrete questions. Would you like me to tell you that one of the things I like most is to rub a woman's sex when she is dressed, something which disgusts me when she is naked. I am astonished that none of you have . . . your . . . [2]

ANDRÉ BRETON I'd say that that's a poor way of posing the question.

JEAN GENBACH Which question?

ANDRÉ BRETON The sexual question.

JEAN GENBACH I don't think one asks oneself such questions.

MARCEL DUHAMEL Shame is something false. And shame is the only question here.

JEAN GENBACH You all know very well that sexuality does not exist.

ANDRÉ BRETON I protest. I don't know that. Sexuality is a word like any other, which can be defined in the dictionary.

JEAN GENBACH I believe the opposite.

ANDRÉ BRETON Then that is purely and simply a matter of shame and inhibition. Rubbing a woman's sex – that's not a sexual phenomenon to you?

JEAN GENBACH It's a phenomenon of love.

ANDRÉ BRETON This is the first time in these debates that someone has been deliberately obstructive. There is no way to continue. All your Monts St.-Michel, your distracted Virgins, only interest me in terms of your sexuality. If I merely found them picturesque, I'd consider myself a fantasist.

MARCEL DUHAMEL You desire a woman. How is this desire manifest?

JEAN GENBACH I never say: 'I desire a woman.' I say: 'I desire Florine Artus who lives at such and such an address.' This need to mean something, to define . . .

MARCEL DUHAMEL The first time you masturbated, were you thinking of a woman?

JEAN GENBACH Yes. I did that during the war before a company of Americans who had had some adventures with factory girls.

MARCEL DUHAMEL Did you love a woman at that moment?

JEAN GENBACH I don't think I can give any particulars, for at that time it wasn't focused precisely on any human beings, as it was three months, one year or ten years later.

PIERRE NAVILLE Do you see any difference between masturbating and making love?

JEAN GENBACH Yes, it's always for lack of . . . .[3] But I prefer to masturbate thinking of a woman I love than to make love with a woman who excites me but whom I don't love.

I like to use a photograph where the woman is naked, or partially naked.

MARCEL DUHAMEL When you make love with a woman, can you induce her orgasm at the moment you choose?

JEAN GENBACH Yes, that always happens.

ANDRÉ BRETON What proportion? What percentage of the time?

JEAN GENBACH Well, I have made love five times in my life, and . . . five times that's what has happened.

MAX MORISE How are you sure?

JEAN GENBACH Because it's easy to see when the woman falls into a certain kind of ecstasy.

ANDRÉ BRETON You trust completely in these signs?

JEAN GENBACH I cannot have any doubts on this subject. That's how it is.

PIERRE NAVILLE Duhamel, when you make love do you always think about whether the woman wants to as much as you?

MARCEL DUHAMEL Not always. To a certain extent I take it into consideration. If the woman has no desire to make love, then it doesn't interest me either. I think one person's desire produces a minimum of desire in the other.

ANDRÉ BRETON, BENJAMIN PÉRET, YVES TANGUY, PIERRE UNIK Absolutely not!

MARCEL DUHAMEL No, you're right, that completely wrong. I see that now.

PIERRE NAVILLE Up to what age do you think a man can have pleasure with a woman?

MARCEL DUHAMEL I think . . . it isn't possible to lay down an age. No idea.

YVES TANGUY I would push the limit back as far as possible.

ANDRÉ BRETON At least until his death.

PIERRE UNIK When you love a woman, Genbach, do you try to show your love immediately?

JEAN GENBACH Yes, immediately, if possible by taking her breasts in my hands.

PIERRE NAVILLE Does Unik mean physical demonstrations only?

JEAN GENBACH I don't think there is any other kind.

PIERRE NAVILLE I cannot precisely define the exact moment when I love a woman. But subsequently there is a moment when I show I love her, I don't know how or why.

YVES TANGUY If you have a desire when you are awake, can you direct your dreams accordingly?

ANDRÉ BRETON Impossible. But with luck I have been able to get things in dreams that I cannot get in reality. All in all, it's somewhat better. It seems there is a kind of compensation.

PIERRE NAVILLE Are you repelled by the idea of making love to a woman who is not white?

MARCEL DUHAMEL It has never happened to me, but I don't think I would find it repugnant.

ANDRÉ BRETON With any non-white woman, so long as it is not a negress.

PIERRE NAVILLE Is that a purely physical repugnance?

ANDRÉ BRETON Yes, and also there's the idea of children, something which is always possible.

YVES TANGUY Naville, have you ever thought of the possibility of a child in such circumstances?

PIERRE NAVILLE Never.

ANDRÉ BRETON Has Genbach been to a brothel?

JEAN GENBACH Yes.

ANDRÉ BRETON Did you make love?

JEAN GENBACH Yes.

MAX MORISE How many times?

JEAN GENBACH Three times. I have also made love on two occasions with a woman I loved. And that is precisely the distinction I'm making.

PIERRE NAVILLE Genbach, if a woman loves you passionately and approaches you, would you submit to her?

JEAN GENBACH That happened to me yesterday. A woman came up and said to me: 'I like your tie; I'd like to suck your cock.'

ANDRÉ BRETON Did you accept?

JEAN GENBACH Naturally.

ANDRÉ BRETON You don't call that making love?

JEAN GENBACH No, I call that a small pleasure which I gave to the woman.

ANDRÉ BRETON Has this happened to you often?

JEAN GENBACH Yes, at Plombières, with old Catérisé.

MAX MORISE You haven't slept with her?

JEAN GENBACH Yes, I did what she wanted, but I don't call that making love.

ANDRÉ BRETON A matter of pure philanthropy, then?

JACQUES PRÉVERT What do you call making love?

JEAN GENBACH It's when I myself, of my own free will, go and find a woman . . . . It's an entirely different motivation.

PIERRE NAVILLE If I requested in my will that you, Genbach, made love to my corpse, would you do it?

JEAN GENBACH Certainly.

MARCEL DUHAMEL Would you prefer to make love with this old woman or with a corpse?

JEAN GENBACH With the corpse, so long as nobody knew about it, so long as it remained a dark secret.

ANDRÉ BRETON The woman you love has died. Never having possessed her, it would be easy for you to possess her now she is dead. Would you do so?

JEAN GENBACH I don't think so. I would, for example, kiss her sex in adoration, to make her a mummy or a pharaoh.

MARCEL DUHAMEL You have told me that your first sexual memory dates from the war. Was that your very first sexual memory?

JEAN GENBACH Yes. I loved one of my aunts, when I was very young. I have a vague predilection for a memory of women's breasts like a pillow. I can't bear to see a woman from behind, When a woman asks me to caress her back, or kiss her bottom . . . I can't bear bottoms.

ANDRÉ BRETON Not very diabolical. And you, do you like being kissed on the bottom, for example?

JEAN GENBACH No.

ANDRÉ BRETON Less and less diabolical.

JEAN GENBACH I think that conception is entirely false. It's a way of anthropomorphising the devil.

MARCEL DUHAMEL What do you think of black masses?

JEAN GENBACH It must be done in solitude, two or three times, and I hate the idea of anything coarse in that domain.

MARCEL DUHAMEL What do you call coarse?

JEAN GENBACH Bestiality, for example.

ANDRÉ BRETON In short, you hate black masses.

JEAN GENBACH No. I repeat that I don't share the usual views on these subjects. A priest can hold a black mass alone with a woman.

ANDRÉ BRETON That is simply sacrilege, it is not a black mass.

So here we have a satanic character who is opposed to sabbatic kisses, black masses, etc.

JEAN GENBACH I loathe all bestiality.

PIERRE NAVILLE What do you think about the succubus?

JEAN GENBACH It's a concrete thing which happens regularly.

ANDRÉ BRETON Explain yourself.

JEAN GENBACH For example, I masturbate while thinking of a woman.

ANDRÉ BRETON We are talking about the succubus, which has nothing to do with that.

JEAN GENBACH It is linked.

ANDRÉ BRETON That is merely your opinion. You are against the succubus if you believe that it's onanism.

JEAN GENBACH I do believe that.

ANDRÉ BRETON The succubus is not something imaginary. It is a matter of clearly defined nocturnal occurrences.

JEAN GENBACH I can feel myself driven to onanism in order to please the succubus. I can say that the woman I've just mentioned is a succubus.

ANDRÉ BRETON It is not a matter of a real woman. We do not know them. We do not solicit them. They come, they excite us.

JEAN GENBACH Why wouldn't I know them?

ANDRÉ BRETON You referred to a real woman . . . . It is the same as with ghosts. They must not be confused with living inhabitants of our world. First of all we have to distinguish those who have disappeared. One cannot see real people and ghosts as the same thing.

Confused discussion of ghosts.

ANDRÉ BRETON You don't believe in haunted houses?

JEAN GENBACH Yes . . . . yes, I do. . . . The greatest freedom is possible. I would like someone to prove to me that a woman is really alive.

ANDRÉ BRETON A thoroughgoing materialism . . . .

JEAN GENBACH All existences are the same. Living or not.

ANDRÉ BRETON I am absolutely opposed to that interpretation. Nonetheless, the coefficient of life is variable.

JEAN GENBACH Then I must acknowledge history, events . . . . For example, given my nocturnal reading habits, I have a much more real idea of Lautréamont than of Rimbaud.

ANDRÉ BRETON Take Baudelaire or Poincaré. Are they on the same level? You cannot deny that one of them is alive. A living woman is different from a dead one.

JEAN GENBACH I can't be as categorical as you.

ANDRÉ BRETON The death of a woman you love cannot leave you indifferent. There is no equivalence.

JEAN GENBACH Obviously . . . . I cannot answer systematically.

ANDRÉ BRETON I would not really know how to answer properly either. Which is why we should return to concrete facts. To the most basic facts of love.

Genbach indicates his astonishment at our concern with the concrete, which he takes for confusion.

ANDRÉ BRETON What does Genbach think of the idea of having children?

JEAN GENBACH I never think about it. I must think about it . . . . I must avoid having them at all costs. I don't know why. So as not to continue this farce. So as not to be implicated any more. To stop myself being continually driven mad, I prefer to believe that everything else is a joke.

ANDRÉ BRETON Prévert? You love children? What do you think of the idea of having one?

JACQUES PRÉVERT I'd kill it on the spot.

ANDRÉ BRETON Why? If he was nice?

JACQUES PRÉVERT He wouldn't have time to be nice, I'd kill him before he had the chance.

ANDRÉ BRETON Tanguy?

YVES TANGUY I find the idea odious. I couldn't say why.

ANDRÉ BRETON Duhamel?

MARCEL DUHAMEL I would not want to be responsible for the life of another.

ANDRÉ BRETON Naville?

PIERRE NAVILLE I would find it regrettable.

ANDRÉ BRETON Why?

PIERRE NAVILLE Because it would have no meaning, and would be awkward.

ANDRÉ BRETON Morise?

MAX MORISE I would not want to put myself in the same situation as my father.

PIERRE NAVILLE And Breton?

ANDRÉ BRETON I am absolutely opposed to it. If it ever happened to me despite everything, I would make sure I never met the child. Public Welfare has its uses.

The sad joke which began with my birth must end with my death. Nonetheless, I reserve the right to change my mind. It seems to me to be possible that in a case of passionate love, where by definition all things are thoughtless, the woman's opinion might prevail over mine. Unik?

PIERRE UNIK I would not want to have a child at any cost, because it is immensely disruptive. The existence of a child is something I cannot contemplate without terror, and if I was given the choice of being born and not being born I would choose the latter.

ANDRÉ BRETON It would be a fine thing to see the child protest at his birth. He would get a good kick in the teeth.

PIERRE UNIK I do not wish anyone to live as the consequence of any act of mine. It is the most detestable thing I could do.

ANDRÉ BRETON I am against all notions of responsibility which could be raised in this context.

PIERRE UNIK I do not believe anyone has the right to use the phrase 'to have children'. There are no fathers.

ANDRÉ BRETON Children have no fathers, but some people claim [rights][4] over children in the name of paternity. Duhamel, what do you think of pregnant women?

MARCEL DUHAMEL Absolutely disgusting.

YVES TANGUY I immediately think of Caesarian sections.

PIERRE UNIK I don't like it at all.

JEAN GENBACH It wouldn't disturb me at all, any more than the fact that a woman has bowels in her stomach, were it not for the swollen belly.

ANDRÉ BRETON Naville?

PIERRE NAVILLE I feel pity.

JACQUES PRÉVERT It's comical if she's ugly, but it's sad if she's beautiful.

ANDRÉ BRETON Very good.

PIERRE UNIK How do you envisage the idea of becoming impotent?

ANDRÉ BRETON It would fill me with the deepest despair.

YVES TANGUY Very sad.

JEAN GENBACH It is an idea I cannot think about. I cannot accept any hypothesis which diminishes me.

ANDRÉ BRETON Death?

PIERRE NAVILLE I don't think of it.

ANDRÉ BRETON What does Unik think of woman's periods?

PIERRE UNIK I've always tried not to think about it, for I find it distressing.

ANDRÉ BRETON What do you think about making love in such circumstances?

JACQUES PRÉVERT Why?

PIERRE UNIK I find the idea violently disgusting.

ANDRÉ BRETON For material or moral reasons?

PIERRE UNIK Moral reasons. It is the very image of physical infirmity, physical degradation.

ANDRÉ BRETON Morise?

MAX MORISE It's something I know nothing about in practice, which I've never thought about because it does not bother me. I would not make love with a woman who had a period.

ANDRÉ BRETON Why?

MAX MORISE Because it isn't clean.

ANDRÉ BRETON What is dirty about it?

MAX MORISE (*Silence*).
ANDRÉ BRETON Naville?
PIERRE NAVILLE Etiquette would suggest there is a right period for everything.
ANDRÉ BRETON Would you make love to a woman who had a period?
PIERRE NAVILLE I'm not answering that.
PIERRE UNIK Tanguy?
YVES TANGUY I find it very pleasant.
ANDRÉ BRETON Why?
YVES TANGUY A matter of colour and smell.
ANDRÉ BRETON Duhamel?
MARCEL DUHAMEL I don't like it because of the sanitary towels and all that.
ANDRÉ BRETON Why do you dislike them so much?
MARCEL DUHAMEL Because of the hospital associations – blood-stained towels and so on. Not that it always stops me making love with a woman.
ANDRÉ BRETON Genbach?
JEAN GENBACH A thing which vexes me is the fact that woman urinate and defecate like men. I didn't know until two years ago that woman had periods. And then it disgusted me. I felt I'd been tricked.
ANDRÉ BRETON But now that you know?
JEAN GENBACH I don't believe that a woman I love can have periods.
JACQUES PRÉVERT It's a very pretty adornment.

It doesn't make any difference, you might as well ask me whether I'd make love to a woman wearing a blouse.

ANDRÉ BRETON It does not make any difference. However, I don't believe it is possible to make love with a woman throughout her period. For several hours there is a material obstacle and also the impossibility of a satisfactory psychological rapport.

What does Genbach think of the idea of Bataille, who, wanting to hurt someone he loathed, had obtained from his mistress . . . .[5]

JEAN GENBACH I can't understand where Bataille saw the revenge in that. I have no very firm views on sperm.
ANDRÉ BRETON Unik?
PIERRE UNIK A refined and splendid vengeance. In Bataille's place, I'd never have had the courage.
ANDRÉ BRETON Can you identify with this person?

MARCEL DUHAMEL Yes.

YVES TANGUY No.

PIERRE NAVILLE I find it all too uncertain to be decisive. He doesn't really seem to have achieved his goal.

MAX MORISE I find it beautiful in the way that something completely barbaric can be beautiful.

ANDRÉ BRETON I think it is wonderful. For me it is one of the very few stories which deals with absolute trust, with the greatest proof of love which a woman can give a man.

PIERRE UNIK What do you think of sensuality, Breton, and how would you define it?

ANDRÉ BRETON It only interests me in a purely cerebral way. I would define it as the only means of producing an imaginative vision, a complete satisfaction, and I refuse to conceive of imagination in any other form (sexual symbolism). I am absolutely opposed to all displays of physical sensuality.[6] The story of 'The Crimson Curtain'.[7] What would you do in such a case?

Jacques Prévert, *circa* 1925. (Collection Madame G. Duhamel)

Fifth Session

7, 17 OR 27 FEBRUARY 1928

Maxime Alexandre

André Breton

Marcel Duhamel

Max Ernst

M.[1]

Marcel Noll

Benjamin Péret

Jacques Prévert

Raymond Queneau

Georges Sadoul

Pierre Unik

MAX ERNST Having read some extracts from the transcripts of the earlier meetings, I would like to give my view of women's orgasms. In my opinion, everything depends on the trust one has in the woman's love. I believe I have observed in some women a genuine orgasm which was a result, not of the sexual act itself, but of what followed it (words, for example).

ANDRÉ BRETON I would say that this is still a subjective approach to the observation of phenomena, as several of us tried to show.

MAX ERNST On the third question (simultaneity of orgasm), it is something I have always wished for in love. Only once have I been able to observe this with certainty, though still subjectively, and it gave me the fullest satisfaction. If you were to ask me for percentages, I would say one in two thousand. Men have a particular way of reaching orgasm. Depraved men want to come again once they have come. They delay ejaculation after reaching their first orgasm. They hold it back. A matter of a tenth of a second, perhaps. I come before ejaculation, perhaps a few seconds before.

MARCEL NOLL You come before ejaculation?

MAX ERNST Orgasm precedes ejaculation.

ANDRÉ BRETON That's a personal, subjective definition of orgasm. As soon as orgasm can be felt, ejaculation cannot, so to speak, be delayed.

MAX ERNST This is one of the most acute problems of our time. *By living more consciously*, one can become precisely aware of the most propitious moment.

ANDRÉ BRETON Yet you have only achieved the desired result once in two thousand times.

BENJAMIN PÉRET For me, there is no orgasm until ejaculation.

MAXIME ALEXANDRE Orgasm is reached before ejaculation but it cannot be reached without ejaculation.

MAX ERNST That's a question of physiology. I have observed that Maxime Alexandre and I do not have the same physique.

MAXIME ALEXANDRE For me, orgasm without ejaculation is impossible.

MAX ERNST There is only one physical exception. In dreams, ejaculation and orgasm coincide.

ANDRÉ BRETON That's not true for me.

BENJAMIN PÉRET Nor for me.

RAYMOND QUENEAU I agree.

MAX ERNST Further to what I've just said about the simultaneity in dreams of orgasm and ejaculation, I have observed that in those circumstances I can reach orgasm without ejaculating, but when I do ejaculate, orgasm comes at the same instant.

ANDRÉ BRETON I am a little unsure how you can determine this by relying on something so precarious as the memory of dreams.

MAX ERNST Up to now I have had the impression of waking up at the moment of orgasm and ejaculating at the same time.

ANDRÉ BRETON Merely an illusion, in my view. From my own experience, I think I wake up at the point ejaculation has finished. One can tell by the position of the sex at that moment: a sensation of dampness, cold or warmth.

MARCEL DUHAMEL, MAXIME ALEXANDRE I don't think that's true.

BENJAMIN PÉRET I've often had the impression that there is a very short space of time between orgasm and ejaculation.

ANDRÉ BRETON Do you think that ejaculation is finished at the moment one awakes?

BENJAMIN PÉRET No, I wake up in the middle of ejaculation.

MAX ERNST On the contrary, I ejaculate, I reach orgasm at the moment the dream dissolves, when I wake up.

RAYMOND QUENEAU I think I wake up just before ejaculation, or I don't wake up at all.

MAXIME ALEXANDRE I only wake up afterwards.

ANDRÉ BRETON I would repeat that, given the unreliability of memory where dreams are concerned, and the diversity of answers, there is no point is pursuing this.

MARCEL DUHAMEL Every time that I have woken up, it is the memory of orgasm which has woken me.

ANDRÉ BRETON I would argue that something else tends to prevent ejaculation continuing when one wakes up, and that is that orgasm ceases. If it carried on, it would provide us with the most precious information on the relationship between dream and reality.

MAX ERNST I've said that I usually reach orgasm at the moment the dream dissolves. The desire to come replaces the dream. Ejaculation takes place. Not long ago I ejaculated in circumstances entirely contrary to my sexual constitution, physiologically and psychologically. In a dream I was buggering a man, and I awoke just at the point of greatest pleasure. As my excitement grew, I pictured all the complexes that might arise from the fact of coming through buggering a fully-clothed man sitting on my knee – as a matter of fact it was a very specific gentleman, whom I don't wish to name. I continued, awake, until I ejaculated. This is a man who, in waking life, disgusts me physically, morally, and from every other point of view.

ANDRÉ BRETON Max Ernst says that for him the desire for orgasm can replace the dream. I would ask what place the will can have in the dream and in the very particular state of confusion which immediately follows it. Furthermore, I think that the anecdote related by Max Ernst raises absolutely only one problem, which is that of the incubus for the man and the succubus for the woman.

RAYMOND QUENEAU, MARCEL NOLL Quite right.

MAX ERNST I believe that a man can very easily be a succubus in dreams.

ANDRÉ BRETON It's as if an incubus got the wrong address.

MAX ERNST Exactly.

RAYMOND QUENEAU I want to add that I don't believe I've ever ejaculated in a dream without some masturbatory desire, but on the other hand I have had orgasms in dreams without ejaculation.

MAX ERNST I agree.

MAXIME ALEXANDRE I've often thought before going to sleep that I would have an orgasm in my dreams. But most of the time I haven't in fact had such an orgasm.

ANDRÉ BRETON I agree with Queneau. I am sure there can be orgasm in a dream without ejaculation.

MAX ERNST, MARCEL DUHAMEL So am I.

ANDRÉ BRETON (2) I repeat my question as to whether one can voluntarily introduce masturbatory or other desires into the dream. (3) To my great regret, I don't believe it is possible to make waking images or desires continue into the dream. I have tried many times.

RAYMOND QUENEAU When there is masturbatory desire, obviously one comes out of the dream, one is awake. When there's orgasm in the dream, one doesn't come out of it, and there may not be ejaculation.

MARCEL DUHAMEL There can also be ejaculation without the slightest orgasm.

MAX ERNST, ANDRÉ BRETON I disagree with that.

ANDRÉ BRETON If there was masturbatory desire one would come out of the dream, that is why there is no masturbatory desire in the dream. Would Queneau give any credence to what I think are deplorable theories which claim that the rubbing of a sheet, or some other physical cause, can produce orgasm, with or without ejaculation?

RAYMOND QUENEAU Yes, I would give credence to that theory.

ANDRÉ BRETON Materialism.

MARCEL DUHAMEL, BENJAMIN PÉRET, MAX ERNST, MARCEL NOLL (*Similar objections.*)

MAX ERNST Anti-surrealist.

MAXIME ALEXANDRE To raise the matter of masturbatory desire before sleep is to abandon the question we were dealing with. I would argue that this desire is incapable of producing orgasm or ejaculation.

MAX ERNST I think we have to some extent been going round the question. Waking and the ending of the dream do not necessarily coincide. Waking, that is to say the replacement of the unconscious will by the conscious will, does not undermine the reality of the phenomenon of orgasm; the phenomena produced by consciousness and the unconscious are too thoroughly intertwined for me to make a precise distinction. I would rather return to the problem of the coincidence of orgasm and ejaculation. The observation that in a dream I ejaculated and had an orgasm simultaneously, in what seemed rather like a waking state, is proof for me that a state exists which is neither one nor the other, something which could be defined as a surrealist state.

ANDRÉ BRETON The differences between us on this subject derive from the fact that some believe their memory is deficient and others claim it is not deficient. This is a question which concerns the dream, and not sexuality.

RAYMOND QUENEAU When and in what circumstances did those here lose their virginity? Péret?

BENJAMIN PÉRET When I was about thirteen or fourteen with the girl next door whose flat was connected to my parents' via a balcony. I only had to get through the dividing railings to find myself in this little girl's bedroom. The first time I tried I was unsuccessful. I had a great deal of difficulty accomplishing the sexual act.

RAYMOND QUENEAU Unik?

PIERRE UNIK I don't remember.

BENJAMIN PÉRET I am amazed that Unik cannot remember the age or the circumstances. It's not as if it were so long ago!

ANDRÉ BRETON I suggest that we no longer consult Unik on any subject throughout this session.

General agreement.

PIERRE UNIK I insist that I don't remember.

ALL That's not true.

MARCEL DUHAMEL At sixteen. With a woman I met on the boulevard de la Madeleine who took me to a brothel in rue de Sèze. Dreadful feeling of disillusion.

BENJAMIN PÉRET Non-accomplishment of the sexual act the first time exacerbated my desire.

MAXIME ALEXANDRE At eighteen. I was with a young man who was older than I and we picked up a woman. We went to a park. We were both caressing her. I was very excited. I didn't have a room. We went to my friend's. I made love with her first. There was a great storm outside. Then my friend made love to her. I was quite impressed by how physically powerful my friend was, compared to me. I was far too excited or carried away to feel either disillusion or satisfaction. Basically, I felt pleased that I had begun.

PIERRE UNIK I retract my first statement. It was when I was between fifteen and sixteen, in a brothel. I visited the brothel four or five times in this period and I've never been back since.

ANDRÉ BRETON I still find it strange that this event left you with no particular strong emotional impression.

MARCEL DUHAMEL I find it strange that this has not forced Unik to re-examine his memory.

Approval from Max Ernst.

MARCEL NOLL I agree.

ANDRÉ BRETON If Unik agrees on this point, let us lift the . . . .[2]

JACQUES PRÉVERT I lost my virginity at thirteen with a woman in a passageway at the Lycée Fénelon. The woman was filthy (there was a picture of Carpentier[3] on a postcard pinned to the wall). I felt . . . .[4]

MARCEL NOLL I was about to turn twenty. During a wedding reception I got to know a very distant cousin (this was after the armistice) who was living in Paris, and whom I suppose I had chosen for the purpose.

On my first visit to Paris in 1920 (?), I went to look her up, at the place where she was staying. I was extremely timid, I remember feeling painfully embarrassed. But great satisfaction the day after.

RAYMOND QUENEAU On 18 March 1919 I was walking near Les Halles in Le Havre. It was raining; I let myself get picked up by a woman who had an umbrella. I went back with her for I had a great desire to make love, if I can put it like that. She didn't even get undressed for it, which greatly annoyed me, but basically I was very pleased.

MAX ERNST At fifteen years, one month and three days, on 14 May 1906. The external circumstances were more interesting than anything that had gone before. With a woman I admired, called Alma, in a forest. A degree of disappointment compared to earlier masturbation (fantasies). Great satisfaction from a physical, and a mental, point of view. At the time I was greatly influenced by my friend: I enjoyed telling him about it.[5]

GEORGES SADOUL At seventeen or eighteen, in the month of July, in the fields, in the suburbs, in a kind of ditch in the grass, with a young woman I'd already been going out with for a few months. She was a virgin, too. A very unpleasant feeling, caused chiefly by the fact that she was a virgin.

M. At eighteen. Through acquaintances. A woman who was the friend of one of my friends' mistresses. No great feeling of disgust, but practically speaking a sense of disillusion.

ANDRÉ BRETON At nineteen. With a young typist from Underwood's who was living in Aubervilliers (I was living in Pantin). I made love with her in a hotel in rue de la Harpe. Throughout the night I was in torment over my physical capacity, although I made love with her four times. Nonetheless, a wonderful feeling, but at 8 a.m. the next day, I was rushed to hospital with acute appendicitis(?).[6]

Apart from this event, what sexual memory has left the strongest emotional impression?

MAXIME ALEXANDRE The most acute memory is of a brothel, when I was twenty or twenty-one. A summer afternoon. The woman was mending her black stockings. I made love with her three or four times. I cannot for the life of me say why that time was the most significant.

MARCEL DUHAMEL One night I was making love with a woman I loved, and it seemed to me that I could go on making love for ever.

GEORGES SADOUL (1) The second time I made love with the same woman as my first time. It was in a bedroom, with nothing to restrict us. (2) While with a woman I liked enormously and desired very much I felt faint and I bit her violently on her lower lip. Then we went out and spent an hour in the countryside without saying or doing anything.

Sensations of the highest order only – if that makes any sense at all.

MAX ERNST A night I spent having failed to go to bed with a woman whom I believed I loved violently. After seeing her again I realised this was a profound error (1921).

RAYMOND QUENEAU The first time I spent a whole night in bed with a woman. I think this is to do with vanity.

BENJAMIN PÉRET It was a day when I was in a kitchen or a toilet (if I could remember precisely, I'd be a real blockhead), and I dreaded or desired that someone would come in.

GEORGES SADOUL I'd like to correct what I said earlier. The second of the two memories is by far the more intense.

MARCEL NOLL It was in a brothel. I was very tired, I met someone with whom I made love and then I realised that she was indisposed. This excited me so much that I began again and it was then that I discovered my favourite way of making love.

BENJAMIN PÉRET I have two memories with more or less equal weight. The first is of making love in the parc de Procé in Nantes with a woman I'd known since the evening before. The second was the night of 14 December 1925 with a woman I'd known for some time, who was drunk.

ANDRÉ BRETON A memory composed of various sexual failures, some almost intentional, with women I loved. The first time was in a field in Nantes and I did not want to make love in this field. The last time was in a hotel room in Lyons and I would have very much liked to make love in that room at that moment.

MAX ERNST Are you monogamous? That's to say, do you believe there is a woman who is your destiny, to the exclusion of all others?

ANDRÉ BRETON Naturally.

MAX ERNST, GEORGES SADOUL, MARCEL NOLL Yes, without any doubt.

PIERRE UNIK Yes. (*Doubtful.*)

RAYMOND QUENEAU No, never. (*Becomes heated.*) No woman could satisfy me or make me monogamous. And I don't give a shit!

ANDRÉ BRETON I protest at that last word.

MAX ERNST And so do I.

MARCEL DUHAMEL (*Shares Queneau's opinion.*)

ANDRÉ BRETON In my view that is the most absolute denial of love.

BENJAMIN PÉRET, MARCEL NOLL, MAX ERNST (*Agreement.*)

RAYMOND QUENEAU I don't see why.

ANDRÉ BRETON Too bad for you. And that's my response to your interjection.

MAXIME ALEXANDRE I have only loved one woman in my life and I only love one woman in my life.

BENJAMIN PÉRET Prévert?

JACQUES PRÉVERT Absolutely, entirely, monogamous with a capital M.

MAX ERNST Let me clarify. Monogamous means: 'Do you believe first and foremost in a destiny?' If you are a surrealist, you believe in a destiny.

ANDRÉ BRETON I object to that last phrase.

MAXIME ALEXANDRE One could say more clearly: 'Have you met a woman who was destined for you?' I have met her.

MARCEL DUHAMEL I think it is impossible to answer.

ALL Why?

MARCEL DUHAMEL (*Silence.*)

RAYMOND QUENEAU Until now, I have not met any woman with whom I could live. Perhaps it could happen to me, but I feel absolutely certain I shall never meet anyone.

JACQUES PRÉVERT No one can object to that.

ANDRÉ BRETON I can!

MAXIME ALEXANDRE So can I.

ANDRÉ BRETON I do not know if I have met this woman. If I have met her, she is not lost to me. And otherwise I am sure I will meet her.

MAXIME ALEXANDRE I have met this woman and I am sure that I have lost her.

BENJAMIN PÉRET I have not met her but it is my greatest hope that I will meet her.

RAYMOND QUENEAU Congratulations to Péret for his optimism.

ANDRÉ BRETON And commiserations to Prévert for his pessimism.

BENJAMIN PÉRET It is my only optimism.

MARCEL NOLL I am absolutely sure that I will meet her. Everything I do is based on that hope.

GEORGES SADOUL I believe I have met this woman and have lost her. My only hope is to find her again in another. (I cannot express this properly.)

MAXIME ALEXANDRE Following on from what Noll said, all my actions are based on my loss.

MAX ERNST I really wonder why some people carry on living – Queneau, for example. I'd gladly make them a present of a length of rope.

RAYMOND QUENEAU I would happily die for love or for the revolution, but I know very well that I'll never encounter either of them.

ANDRÉ BRETON A remark which is typically counter-revolutionary and typically anti-love.

PIERRE UNIK I don't think one can talk of positivism in relation to what Queneau has said.

RAYMOND QUENEAU Any kind of confidence in life seems to me to be anti-surrealist.

ANDRÉ BRETON In which case I am against surrealism as Queneau understands it.

BENJAMIN PÉRET I completely agree with Breton, it's only meaning I give to surrealism.

[. . .][7]

MAXIME ALEXANDRE I think entirely the opposite to Queneau.

ANDRÉ BRETON The question must have been put badly. It is not a matter of having confidence in life. Our own non-conformism is a kind of answer to that. Yet there is one thing alone in life which is not denied and forbidden to us, and that is love.

JACQUES PRÉVERT Against.[8]

MAX ERNST And hope in emotion.

JACQUES PRÉVERT There is nothing, and there is nothing more to be said.

BENJAMIN PÉRET Dada.

JACQUES PRÉVERT [. . .] [9] Shit!

ANDRÉ BRETON Once again I must protest at this form of discussion.

PIERRE UNIK I object to the word Dada. It's too facile.

MARCEL DUHAMEL And in that case I am a Dadaist in opposition to Péret.

ANDRÉ BRETON I entirely agree with Péret's intervention, which was extremely perceptive and absolutely correct.

Agreement from Max Ernst and Maxime Alexandre.

RAYMOND QUENEAU I disagree. The reigning optimism among some of surrealism's personalities seems to me quite astonishing. For myself, I have no hope in anything. But to answer the question . . .

MAXIME ALEXANDRE Still Dada!

RAYMOND QUENEAU . . . to answer the charge of Dadaism, I would say that surrealism and love and the revolution seem to me to represent all that is best in the world.

MAX ERNST I note a flagrant contradiction in what Queneau is saying . . .

PIERRE UNIK Absolutely not.

MAX ERNST On the one hand he allies himself with bourgeois scepticism in its opposition to love (which for me is the same thing as revolution), while on the other hand he retains a degree of optimism towards love.

RAYMOND QUENEAU To accuse me first of bourgeois scepticism and then of a degree of optimism towards love strikes me as revealing considerable confidence in bourgeois logic.

ANDRÉ BRETON I would like to ask Queneau what logic he intends to substitute for bourgeois logic.

RAYMOND QUENEAU None at all.

ANDRÉ BRETON So how would you reply without logic to such questions?

RAYMOND QUENEAU Through a degree of trust in people I consider my friends, without any sentimentality.

ANDRÉ BRETON That is impossible.

RAYMOND QUENEAU I understand friendship in the same way I understand love. I can conceive of love apart from this destiny that people are trying to impose on me.

MAX ERNST What 'people'? Do you mean God?

RAYMOND QUENEAU I've no idea. The fact is that questions have been asked about destiny in love which I neither understand nor wish to understand.

ANDRÉ BRETON Again, it's a question of vocabulary: 'destiny' stands for something else. Does Queneau think that the goal of love is love for its own sake or love of a human being?

RAYMOND QUENEAU For me, it is love of a human being.

MAX ERNST Contradictory.

ANDRÉ BRETON And is this human being real?

RAYMOND QUENEAU That is what I think.

I will never meet her, of course.

PIERRE UNIK This view does not seem at all tainted with positivism to me.

ANDRÉ BRETON Queneau has never been accused of wholehearted positivism. We have been responding to his perhaps unthinking accusation of optimism.

MAX ERNST What do you think of marriage, Péret?

BENJAMIN PÉRET It is of no great interest to me. I sometimes think about it as a possibility. I make no distinction between marriage and free union. It goes without saying that if a woman I loved asked me to marry her, I'd do so without hesitation.

MARCEL DUHAMEL Marriage seems to me to be a purely social question, and it doesn't interest me any more or less than any other social question.

GEORGES SADOUL A purely legal matter which is of absolutely no interest to me.[10]

MAXIME ALEXANDRE, MARCEL NOLL, RAYMOND QUENEAU, ANDRÉ BRETON Same opinion.

MAXIME ALEXANDRE I would like to ask about jealousy and possessiveness in love. Péret?

BENJAMIN PÉRET I accept jealousy from the woman. As for me, I suppose I tend to reject it, but not very strongly. I don't really understand the idea of possessiveness.

MARCEL DUHAMEL I strongly reject the idea of possessiveness in love. I have occasionally fallen victim to a moment or two of jealousy. It's more or less a physical feeling. That aside, I am not distressed by the idea that a woman I love could be physically attracted to another man.

PIERRE UNIK To me, jealousy seems quite distinct from possessiveness in love. I am absolutely opposed to possessiveness but I can certainly suffer from jealousy with regard to a woman I love.

ANDRÉ BRETON Which means that you look favourably on the idea of possession.

PIERRE UNIK No. Because I would never demand fidelity from a woman. But despite everything that doesn't mean that I don't feel jealousy.

MARCEL NOLL I don't think I'm susceptible to jealousy in Alexandre's sense. When a woman leaves me I believe that there is nothing I can do but resign myself to it, and I am not master of the feelings which overwhelm me at such a time.

GEORGES SADOUL And if you fall in love with a woman who loves another?

MARCEL NOLL That has never happened to me.

MAXIME ALEXANDRE In love, there is no question for me either of jealousy or possessiveness. They only become issues to the extent that life is imperfect.

PIERRE UNIK I would suggest to Noll that if he can talk of resignation this is because he feel jealousy.

BENJAMIN PÉRET, ANDRÉ BRETON There's absolutely no connection!

ANDRÉ BRETON I am completely immune to jealousy. A woman's jealousy annoys me, but no more than that. As to the idea of possession in love, it is hardly more abject than the idea of any other kind of property.

What does Max Ernst think of cohabiting with the woman he loves?

MAX ERNST You can live with a woman as long as you love her. Given that I respond entirely affirmatively to the 'question of monogamy', I believe it is perfectly possible to live continuously with a woman without love being in any way diminished.

BENJAMIN PÉRET Every time I've loved a woman, I have wanted to live with her and tried to achieve this.

MARCEL DUHAMEL I agree with Max Ernst.

ANDRÉ BRETON Sadoul, how much do you take physical beauty into account in your appreciation of a woman?

GEORGES SADOUL I do not think the woman I love must necessarily be beautiful.

MAXIME ALEXANDRE In love, such a question doesn't even arise.

RAYMOND QUENEAU I take women as I find them.

MARCEL NOLL Beauty is necessarily subjective. The woman you love is always beautiful.

PIERRE UNIK I always think that a woman I love is beautiful.

ANDRÉ BRETON That's not what I meant.

MAX ERNST Our ideas of beauty are too fixed (for me, it is the Venus de Milo) for objective beauty to play any decisive role in sexuality.

BENJAMIN PÉRET I am always attracted to some particular outward physical feature in a woman – something I find exceptionally appealing. That will usually be enough to make her beautiful in my eyes.

ANDRÉ BRETON I do not think the question has been properly covered at all. Contemplation of a woman's physical beauty is the most important thing in the world. A woman can be a genius, can embody all the mental qualities I hold dear, yet all it takes is one single physical detail which displeases me for me to lose all interest.

MAX ERNST If a woman was morally and intellectually despicable but was the most beautiful woman in the world, would she interest you?

ANDRÉ BRETON Naturally not, but I would have taken the trouble to evaluate her from a moral and intellectual point of view, whereas a less beautiful woman would not have made me curious.

MAX ERNST In that case, beauty plays a decisive role as a starting-point?

ANDRÉ BRETON Naturally.

BENJAMIN PÉRET Naturally.

Antonin Artaud as Marat in Abel Gance's *Napoléon*, 1925.

Sixth Session

3 MARCH 1928

Antonin Artaud

André Breton

Marcel Duhamel

Benjamin Péret

Jacques Prévert

Raymond Queneau

Yves Tanguy

Pierre Unik

ANTONIN ARTAUD I tend to see the realm of sexuality as personal, as something quite individual and private. I enter into it, as I do all life's experiences, but expect nothing. The conclusions that I can draw from it by myself seem to be more fruitful, or could be more fruitful for others, according to the circumstances and the manner in which I formulate them. In investigations like this one, for most people a degree of ostentation inevitably intrudes. There is thus also the problem of whether such an investigation can distinguish between people who are being sincere and those who are not. Sexuality in itself I find repulsive. I would gladly do without it. I only wish all mankind had reached that point. I am sick and tired of being a slave to these filthy urges. Nevertheless, I acknowledge that in some cases one can abandon oneself to sexuality as to a kind of death – though this is a form of despair which can hardly be recommended.

Péret, is sexuality of great importance in your life? How far is your mind tainted by it?

BENJAMIN PÉRET It's of very great importance to me and has a strong influence on my ideas.

ANTONIN ARTAUD Could it divert you from particular aims or actions? Faced with a sexual desire and a significant desire of another nature, which would you choose, assuming of course that both occurred at the same time?

BENJAMIN PÉRET A sexual desire holds no interest for me unless it is accompanied by love, and for love I would leave everything.

ANTONIN ARTAUD You're jumping into a different realm.

BENJAMIN PÉRET The two are intimately linked.

ANTONIN ARTAUD If one can bring love into an investigation of sexuality, the investigation is pointless.

ANDRÉ BRETON Why do you wish to separate them?

ANTONIN ARTAUD Because otherwise you confuse everything. My question concerned sexuality alone. I'll rephrase it: 'In a case where there is no question of love and where you are faced with a sexual desire and another kind of desire, which of the two would Breton choose?'

ANDRÉ BRETON The second, naturally. But I still believe we must begin by linking the question of sexuality to that of love. The whole point of this investigation is, in love, to establish what part belongs to sexuality.

ANTONIN ARTAUD Have you never in your life experienced great sexual pleasure without any surge of love and with only a slight, probably physical attraction to the woman in question?

ANDRÉ BRETON I have never so to speak experienced sexual 'pleasure'. I may not have been certain of loving every woman with whom I've made love, but I've been far less certain of not loving her.

ANTONIN ARTAUD In speaking of sexual pleasure, Breton, are you only thinking of the physical aspect, or do you never think of the physical aspect, or is it that in the sexual act the mental pleasure you experience encompasses everything?

ANDRÉ BRETON I cannot conceive of any pleasure except normal pleasure.

ANTONIN ARTAUD That answer seems to me extraordinarily tendentious and arbitrary.

ANDRÉ BRETON Why?

ANTONIN ARTAUD We do not agree about a single word we're saying. If we have to analyse every word, any discussion will be impossible.

ANDRÉ BRETON There must have been a misunderstanding over the sense of the word *pleasure*. If we are talking about orgasm in the strict sense, then I have no objection to taking the most objective approach.

JACQUES PRÉVERT How long do you think you can go without making love?

ANTONIN ARTAUD Years.

JACQUES PRÉVERT I agree entirely.

YVES TANGUY Me too.

BENJAMIN PÉRET For me that would be impossible.

ANDRÉ BRETON So for you it is not necessarily a question of love, since you are ready to bow to psychological[1] impulses.

BENJAMIN PÉRET A gap of several years seems to me to be pure fantasy. I cannot conceive a priori that I could spend such a long time without making love. I am not looking for love-making, I am looking for a woman.

JACQUES PRÉVERT It's the same thing.

ANDRÉ BRETON It is not the same thing. The choice which rules over love can be exercised in those conditions.

ANTONIN ARTAUD Being absolutely honest with himself, can Péret swear that it is not an idea of sexuality which has motivated him prior to any particular female representation?

BENJAMIN PÉRET It is always hope in the woman I meet that leads me to want to know her.

ANDRÉ BRETON That's really very vague.[2] One could reply to Artaud that it is irrelevant to know whether in such a case it is an idea of sexuality which drives you, just as it is irrelevant to know whether all the other acts of one's life are inspired by a principle of self-preservation or by the need to propagate the species.

BENJAMIN PÉRET I can only judge a posteriori and I don't know what I'd think on any particular occasion. I obey a kind of attraction.

ANTONIN ARTAUD The responses of Péret and Breton have completely sidetracked the question I was asking. I was not talking about drives buried in the limbo of a species to which I am aware of having ceased to belong, at least in the world as we know it, and I consider that there is always a choice to be made between what are clearly sexual representations. That was the point of my question.

ANDRÉ BRETON There is no state of sexual need analogous to the needs produced by alcohol, tobacco or drugs.

ANTONIN ARTAUD There is indeed an analogous – and vile – need. Between a sexual desire, accompanied by love, which you could immediately satisfy, and an intellectual calling of the highest order which would give you complete mental satisfaction, which would you choose?

BENJAMIN PÉRET Naturally I would choose the former because for me that would be everything.

ANDRÉ BRETON Because for me only that desire accompanied by love can provide complete mental satisfaction.

ANTONIN ARTAUD Prévert?

JACQUES PRÉVERT There could never be any intellectual calling of the highest order which would give me complete mental satisfaction.

YVES TANGUY The former, naturally. I'd be quite incapable of achieving the latter.

PIERRE UNIK What I would have to say has already been very well expressed by Breton.

ANTONIN ARTAUD I knew very well how all those here would answer such a question, and I only asked it in order to convey my own feelings on this matter. I believe that the satisfactions love can provide are always of a rather remote nature and devoid of any kind of certainty. I obstinately maintain my belief in satisfactions of an intellectual order in opposition to love and superior to it because they comprise an idea of possession which is more immediate and more certain. Love carries an idea of submission and depersonalisation which I find intolerable, and I believe I can allow myself to fall into a similar state of rapture to that which others find in love on my own, facing only myself.

ANDRÉ BRETON In answering Artaud's question just now, I overlooked, with some difficulty, his use of the word 'satisfaction'. To me this word suggests certain pragmatic concerns which I do not share in the slightest. If I place love above everything, it is because it is for me the most desperate, the most despairing state of affairs imaginable. My own depersonalisation in this realm is precisely all that I wish for. As to my submission, it is so bound up with domination that I am entirely taken over by it. I can at last lose the feeling of being free for no good reason.

ANTONIN ARTAUD Once again I object to the way people are persisting in giving a highly specific meaning to a word which in this question I was using in its most general sense. I refuse to accept that, habitually and consciously, despair is the dominant emotion when one is seeking or thinking about love. In any case, I consider that the mind conceived in its totality disposes of a far greater despair-inducing capacity than love does.

ANDRÉ BRETON I have never said that despair predominates in love; at most it shapes it. But love is the 'end' of this despair and is thus beyond all the mental resources you speak of.

ANTONIN ARTAUD I would point out to Breton that he said just now that if he placed love above everything it was because for him it was the most desperate and despairing state of things, and that I was thus correct in replying to him that he accorded despair the dominant place in love.

ANDRÉ BRETON I did say that and yet I do not accord despair the dominant place in love. This is because here I am expressing myself outside of love and indeed despairing of love. It's very subjective, if you like.

ANTONIN ARTAUD In that case, perhaps I was mistaken . . .

RAYMOND QUENEAU The other day I was asked: 'Do you believe that there is a woman who is your destiny?' What does Artaud think?

ANTONIN ARTAUD I've never believed anything else. I think it's highly probable that I'll never meet her.

ANDRÉ BRETON What is this virtual notion of destiny? If you are not going to meet this woman, how can you say that she is destined for you?

ANTONIN ARTAUD I will necessarily meet her, but perhaps not in this life. I would add that I have a very low opinion of this woman!

ANDRÉ BRETON I have the very highest opinion of her, not considering myself a free man.

ANTONIN ARTAUD Is the thought of the relations you had had with a woman who has died something which exalts or diminishes your idea of love? Does it enrich the feeling of despair that you seek in the depths of love?

ANDRÉ BRETON I have never had relations with a woman who I know is now dead.

ANTONIN ARTAUD Has anyone had sexual relations with a woman who has since died?

YVES TANGUY Yes.

ANTONIN ARTAUD Has that given you any pangs of remorse?

YVES TANGUY Oh! No, well . . . .

ANTONIN ARTAUD I can assure you that that has terrified me and paralysed me for the rest of my life.

Does anyone here find the idea of masturbation loathsome? Has that always been the case, or when did it stop being so, or start to become so.

JACQUES PRÉVERT I've never found it loathsome, I've never had the idea that I was doing something loathsome.

ANDRÉ BRETON Strictly speaking, it has never been loathsome for me. But I've long seen it as a feeble expedient and as something rather wretched, all the more so no doubt in that I accepted the idea that it can be harmful to one's health. It's strange that the more I've come to see it as acceptable, the less I've indulged in it. It did not become completely acceptable to me until the day I learned from a work of Wittels on Freud that certain psychoanalysts of the Zurich school recommend it as therapeutic in some cases. Since then I have only seen it as a cure, and am thus prejudiced against it as I am against cures in general.

MARCEL DUHAMEL Masturbation has never seemed loathsome to me, I indulged in it with relish until I was fourteen; much more rarely since then.

ANTONIN ARTAUD However hard I've tried to convince myself of its legitimacy, I have always found it loathsome; it has always seemed to entail the same kind of diminishment of myself.

BENJAMIN PÉRET It has never seemed loathsome to me, but for a long time now I've deemed it a last resort.

ANDRÉ BRETON It has never felt like a last resort to me, but rather as a mental expedient whenever the sexual act with a woman has not had the usual effectiveness for me.

Exit Artaud.

ANDRÉ BRETON You have not made love for some time. How many times can you do it in one night (from nine in the evening to nine in the morning) and on each of the three following days (from nine in the morning on 3 March to nine in the morning on 6 March)? Can you make love every day? Without any exception? How many times per day? What is the maximum you've managed in twelve hours?

JACQUES PRÉVERT I don't know how many times I *can* make love. Between nine in the evening and nine in the morning means nothing to me. I usually make love once or twice. I hate sport.

BENJAMIN PÉRET In general, three or four times. More or less the same during the next three days. I don't think I could make love every day for a year. Nine times in five hours.

ANDRÉ BRETON (1) Four times. (2) The second day, once or not at all, the third day, two or three times. The fourth, once or twice. Every day? Yes, or more or less, for a fixed period (weeks). Once or twice. Maximum? I have never made love more than five times without feeling an irresistible need to go for a walk, preferably alone.

YVES TANGUY (1) Three times and three times each day for the next three days. Every day? No. Maximum, five times.

RAYMOND QUENEAU (1) Three or four times. The second day, *idem*. The third day? Never happened. Every day? I doubt it. Maximum, four times.

PIERRE UNIK (1) Four times. The next three days? Twice a day. I've never made love three days running. Maximum? Four times.

MARCEL DUHAMEL (1) Three times. The same thing for the next three days. Every day? Yes, once a day, but I don't always want to. Maximum? Eight times.

RAYMOND QUENEAU You have not made love for some time. How long before you ejaculate from the moment you are alone with the woman?

JACQUES PRÉVERT Maybe five minutes, maybe an hour.

MARCEL DUHAMEL *Idem.*

BENJAMIN PÉRET There are two parts. Before the sexual act itself, a period which can be quite long, perhaps half an hour according to my desire at the time. (2) The second part, the sexual act: around five minutes.

ANDRÉ BRETON The first part, a lot longer than half an hour. Almost indefinite. (2) Twenty seconds maximum.

MARCEL DUHAMEL To be more precise, during the second part, a minimum of five minutes.

RAYMOND QUENEAU The preliminary act: maximum twenty minutes. (2) Less than a minute.

YVES TANGUY (1) Two hours. (2) Two minutes.

PIERRE UNIK (1) One hour. (2) Between fifteen and forty seconds.

ANDRÉ BRETON And the second time? Accepting that one makes love in the shortest possible time? Me? Three to five minutes for the sexual act.

BENJAMIN PÉRET The sexual act: around a quarter of an hour.

YVES TANGUY Ten minutes.

MARCEL DUHAMEL *Idem.*

PIERRE UNIK It varies: between two and five minutes.

RAYMOND QUENEAU A quarter of an hour.

JACQUES PRÉVERT Three minutes or even twenty minutes. What do you think of a woman with a shaved sex?

ANDRÉ BRETON Very beautiful, infinitely better. I have never seen it, but it must be magnificent.

Apart from ejaculating in the vagina, mouth or anus, where do you like to ejaculate, in order of preference?

BENJAMIN PÉRET (1) Armpits. (2) Between the breasts. (3) On the stomach.

RAYMOND QUENEAU Between the breasts. Nowhere else.

PIERRE UNIK Between the breasts.

JACQUES PRÉVERT On the back. On the neck. Elsewhere.

YVES TANGUY On the stomach. On the face. In the hair and on the feet.

ANDRÉ BRETON (1) Over the eyes. (2) In the hair.

MARCEL DUHAMEL (1) On the bottom. (2) Between the breasts. (3) Armpits.

ANDRÉ BRETON What would Pierre Unik think of being sodomised by a woman?

PIERRE UNIK I think it would be very good. It has never happened to me. I would find it very exciting.

ANDRÉ BRETON How do you think the woman would do it?

PIERRE UNIK I suppose by introducing her clitoris into my rectum.

BENJAMIN PÉRET I don't share that opinion, it doesn't appeal to me at all.

ANDRÉ BRETON How would she do it?

BENJAMIN PÉRET There are two ways. Either an abnormal development of the clitoris would allow her to do it that way. Or using a dildo.

YVES TANGUY It appeals to me.

MARCEL DUHAMEL It appeals to me very much.

JACQUES PRÉVERT Very appealing. It's never happened to me. Maybe it will happen to me.

ANDRÉ BRETON It does not appeal to me at all at the moment. But what an unusual idea some of us have of the dimensions of even an abnormal clitoris, and of the mechanical capacities of that organ!

What does Queneau think of making love standing up? Has it ever happened to him?

RAYMOND QUENEAU It doesn't appeal to me. It must be exhausting.

MARCEL DUHAMEL It's very appealing, but I don't think I could do it. Isn't the idea of making love standing up (both standing up) liable to deprive you of your capacity to perform?

Unanimous no.

MARCEL DUHAMEL I am sure I would be quite unable to perform.

YVES TANGUY It greatly appeals to me.

BENJAMIN PÉRET I've done it, it's very tiring.

JACQUES PRÉVERT I used to do it often. I don't any more and I regret that.

BENJAMIN PÉRET What do you think of making love in the bath?

JACQUES PRÉVERT I like it very much.

RAYMOND QUENEAU It's an amusing idea.

MARCEL DUHAMEL It must be wonderful, I've never done it.

YVES TANGUY Very good; mainly in sea water.

ANDRÉ BRETON Very appealing in prospect, but very difficult to achieve.

PIERRE UNIK I must try one day.

BENJAMIN PÉRET I've never made love in a bath. I don't really see how it could be done. I've done it in the sea and it's extremely exhausting.

RAYMOND QUENEAU What would you feel about seeing a woman urinate?

ANDRÉ BRETON If it's a woman I love, it could only be very pleasant.

YVES TANGUY Very, very pleasant.

MARCEL DUHAMEL Very exciting.

BENJAMIN PÉRET Very pretty to watch. And pleasantly musical.

RAYMOND QUENEAU It's very good.

JACQUES PRÉVERT I agree.

PIERRE UNIK It's never happened to me.

BENJAMIN PÉRET What does Duhamel think about hearing a woman fart?

MARCEL DUHAMEL It was one of the most unpleasant things I could remember when it happened to me a long time ago. Now, I don't think it would bother me.

RAYMOND QUENEAU No opinion.

JACQUES PRÉVERT The less often the better.

ANDRÉ BRETON Appalled by it.

YVES TANGUY I don't care.

BENJAMIN PÉRET Very unpleasant.

PIERRE UNIK It must be very unpleasant. What part of the woman's body do you most like to kiss?

MARCEL DUHAMEL The mouth.

RAYMOND QUENEAU The nostrils.

ANDRÉ BRETON The breasts.

BENJAMIN PÉRET The ears and the breasts.

YVES TANGUY The legs.

JACQUES PRÉVERT The bottom.

PIERRE UNIK The nape of the neck and the tops of the thighs.

RAYMOND QUENEAU What do you think of rape?

BENJAMIN PÉRET Absolutely opposed to it.
YVES TANGUY Very, very good.
ANDRÉ BRETON Absolutely hostile to it.
RAYMOND QUENEAU It's the only thing that appeals to me.
MARCEL DUHAMEL It doesn't appeal to me.
JACQUES PRÉVERT I find it legitimate.
PIERRE UNIK I am against it.

Jacques-André Boiffard. Photograph by Berenice Abbott.

Seventh Session

6 MAY 1928

Jean Baldensperger

Jacques-A Boiffard[1]

André Breton

Jean Caupenne

Marcel Duhamel

Marcel Noll

Jacques Prévert

Georges Sadoul

Pierre Unik

Y.[2]

JEAN BALDENSPERGER We are going to consider sexual relations apart from those with women, in particular those with animals.

ANDRÉ BRETON We discussed the question of bestiality very briefly in an earlier session. Since everyone present declared their antipathy to it and claimed that they had never had any tendency in this direction, there was no point in pursuing it.

JEAN BALDENSPERGER On the contrary I think we should pursue it, because it provided my introduction to sexual pleasure. I had a female donkey, who is still alive, with whom I had very close relations for a year.[3]

JACQUES PRÉVERT How old was she?

JEAN BALDENSPERGER Two.

JACQUES PRÉVERT And you?

JEAN BALDENSPERGER Fourteen.

ANDRÉ BRETON Will you describe the relations in question as precisely as possible?

JEAN BALDENSPERGER I did it through a shirt. Usually I would harness her, lead her into the woods, then take off the pack part of the harness with the very clear sensation of undressing someone, then indulge my little passions. Afterwards I would re-harness her, and go home.

JACQUES PRÉVERT What was the donkey's attitude to this?

JEAN BALDENSPERGER This is what is so interesting. The first times she was perfectly amenable, but later she would not allow it, except when she was on heat.

JEAN CAUPENNE What position did you adopt? Did you climb up on a stone?

JEAN BALDENSPERGER No, because she was quite small and I was quite tall. It was only later that I discovered you could make yourself come on your own.

ANDRÉ BRETON What kind of emotions did you feel after this act?

JEAN BALDENSPERGER Disgust the first times, along with fear that people at home would find out what I'd done.

ANDRÉ BRETON What led you to choose this particular animal instead of some other one?

JEAN BALDENSPERGER She was the one I saw most often. It was always on Tuesdays and Saturdays before my history lessons, because I was free at that time.

ANDRÉ BRETON What would you think now about doing it again?

JEAN BALDENSPERGER It wouldn't particularly interest me. But it wouldn't disgust me.

PIERRE UNIK Have you never been attracted to any other animals?

JEAN BALDENSPERGER There was a goat once. But that was very rare. I didn't bugger it. This kind of zoophilia is very common in the country.

JEAN CAUPENNE It would be interesting to know whether even those who now find the idea unpleasant have ever had relations with animals.

MARCEL DUHAMEL The only pleasure I've ever had with animals was with little dogs, letting them nip my hand. It never went as far as orgasm.

JEAN BALDENSPERGER A long time ago my brother said to me (he was climbing on to the donkey's back): 'It feels good when I stretch myself out on her.'

(No one else has had relations with animals.)

ANDRÉ BRETON Have Caupenne and Baldensperger any comments to make on the responses that have already been recorded?

JEAN BALDENSPERGER You say that if a woman is dirty it doesn't stop you feeling attracted to her. But I think that cleanliness is one of the basic requirements.

JEAN CAUPENNE Cleanliness is absolutely necessary and elegance preferable.

ANDRÉ BRETON Naturally. But still it doesn't seem to me impossible to love a woman who is dirty and stays dirty, since love has nothing to do with such material considerations. Stupidity in a woman, on the other hand, seems to me to be an intolerable defect. All that I wish is to love a woman enough to love her whether she's clean or dirty.

GEORGES SADOUL, MARCEL DUHAMEL I completely agree. Love is beyond such questions.

JEAN BALDENSPERGER Yes, but when you speak of love you are also thinking of going to bed with her. Would you agree to go to bed with a woman who was in a disgusting state?

ANDRÉ BRETON Definitely.

JEAN BALDENSPERGER I would not be able to make love with a woman whose arse was encrusted with shit.

ANDRÉ BRETON That's your affair. There are people who like that very much (the Marquis de Sade and all the great *érotomanes*). I consider that Baldensperger is talking about this like a child. I don't see any difference between the encrusted shit of the woman one loves and her eyes. Perhaps someone could explain.

JEAN CAUPENNE Shit isn't exactly part of the person, so far as I know.

ANDRÉ BRETON Why not? Of course it is!

PIERRE UNIK These reflections on shit are not interesting.

MARCEL DUHAMEL What do people think of jokes about sexual matters and of scatological jokes?

JACQUES PRÉVERT I think very highly of them, as of all jokes.

GEORGES SADOUL I think they're disgusting.

JEAN CAUPENNE I never connect them with my own sexual life. They're jokes like any others.

PIERRE UNIK Generally, I loathe them. When women tell them I find it absolutely intolerable.

MARCEL DUHAMEL I don't like jokes when they're of a private nature. When they're more wide-ranging (particularly scatological jokes), I can find some very funny. Crude humour is always detestable.
[. . .][4]

ANDRÉ BRETON I find scatological jokes quite funny in some cases. And I'm not against very daring jokes of a sexual nature as long as love itself is not the issue.

What does Baldensperger think of the possibility of simultaneous orgasm?

JEAN BALDENSPERGER It seems to me it's something which happens often enough. In my own case, I'm absolutely sure of it.

ANDRÉ BRETON Why? I myself am sure of the opposite.

JEAN BALDENSPERGER Because of the signs of contractions.

ANDRÉ BRETON Don't you think these signs of contractions can be simulated?

JEAN BALDENSPERGER No. What about you – are you capable of faking orgasm?

ANDRÉ BRETON Perfectly.

JEAN CAUPENNE It must happen, but it doesn't seem very desirable. It is better that the woman comes first.

Marcel Noll enters.

MARCEL NOLL What do you think of masturbation, Baldensperger?

JEAN BALDENSPERGER It's a very normal thing between around fifteen and seventeen, because at that age you have few chances of having relations with a woman.

MARCEL NOLL Why?

JEAN BALDENSPERGER The times I wanted to with them, they found me rather young.

MARCEL NOLL What do you think of the satisfaction or non-satisfaction obtained through masturbation?

JEAN BALDENSPERGER I masturbated as a compensation. It was a lot better with the donkey.

JEAN CAUPENNE His sister was called Ânette.[5]

ANDRÉ BRETON Do you think that from the start masturbation is or is not accompanied by female images?

JEAN BALDENSPERGER For me, it wasn't.

MARCEL NOLL Caupenne?

JEAN CAUPENNE If you masturbate, it's because you can't have a woman for the time being.

MARCEL NOLL Do you still do it?

JEAN CAUPENNE No.

ANDRÉ BRETON And Baldensperger?

JEAN BALDENSPERGER No.

ANDRÉ BRETON Is there anyone who has masturbated in the last six months?

ALL Yes.

JACQUES PRÉVERT Not me.

ANDRÉ BRETON A classic indication of impotence.

MARCEL NOLL When you masturbate, is this followed by a feeling of shame or by complete satisfaction without any kind of moral embarrassment?

JEAN CAUPENNE I don't feel any kind of embarrassment.

MARCEL NOLL Do you think of a particular woman or just any woman?

JEAN CAUPENNE I don't think of a particular woman.

MARCEL NOLL What precisely do you think of?

JEAN CAUPENNE I don't think of the body at all. I believe I think of something which doesn't exist, woman in general.

MARCEL DUHAMEL Every time I've done it, it's been with the aid of an erotic photo or postcard, or by imagining the arse or the buttocks of a woman I may have seen passing in the street.

Y. How do you become aware that you want to make love with a woman, Prévert?

JACQUES PRÉVERT I become aware that I want to make love with a woman, but I don't reflect on it at the time. Seeing a woman in slippers makes me want to make love.

MARCEL DUHAMEL Yes, I find slippers and dressing-gowns exciting.

ANDRÉ BRETON I object to the way Duhamel's response seems to have been influenced by Prévert's. It is impossible for two men to share a taste for something as particular as slippers.

MARCEL DUHAMEL Breton has no right to claim what I say is false. How could he know?

Y. Breton, when do you become aware that you desire a woman?

ANDRÉ BRETON I desire a woman when I love her. This is certainly not accompanied by an erection. If you love a woman, it is absolutely impossible to masturbate while thinking of her, except in very special circumstances. If it happens all the same, there will be interference; other women will come to mind and intervene. There is only one exception, where there has been a formal agreement between the man and the woman. If for example it's been agreed that you'll both masturbate at five o'clock!

JEAN BALDENSPERGER I agree entirely.

ANDRÉ BRETON Flaubert sent his sperm to a woman in a letter. I find that the purest of acts.

MARCEL NOLL What does Prévert think of that story?

JACQUES PRÉVERT I don't know anything about Flaubert. It doesn't interest me.

MARCEL DUHAMEL *A priori*, I want to go to bed with every pretty woman I meet. If I don't do it, it's because I'm afraid of being disappointed.

Y. At what moment do you feel happiest in love, Breton?

ANDRÉ BRETON It's after making love. . . . That's not very clear. . . . I am never happy in love.

JEAN CAUPENNE I don't see what relation that has to possession. It can be before, it can be after.

ANDRÉ BRETON What is possession?

Y. It's the act of making love or even not making love, taking, embracing, I don't know. It's the moment when you feel you belong to the man. It's a matter of the domination of the woman by the man.

ANDRÉ BRETON I would suggest that this is indeed a very particular usage of the word *possession*, which is generally understood to mean what happens at the moment of orgasm.

Y. What sort of sensation do you experience when you come, Duhamel?

MARCEL DUHAMEL I don't think it's possible to explain.

Y. Do you completely lose your senses, as you might, for example, in a disaster?

MARCEL DUHAMEL No.

Y. Can the appearance or the smell of a sex influence your desires when you are making love?

JEAN CAUPENNE In a bad sense, yes. If I'm not disgusted by it in some particular way, then it makes no effective difference.

GEORGES SADOUL A depilated or shaved sex I find completely disgusting.

MARCEL NOLL Hairless sexes are very attractive.

ANDRÉ BRETON It's a scandal that there are still unshaven sexes!

JEAN CAUPENNE What does Noll think of the exchange of swear-words and insults by a man and woman making love?

MARCEL NOLL That's an otiose and uninteresting question.

General protests.

JEAN CAUPENNE It's as interesting as any other sexual obsession.

JEAN BALDENSPERGER In some cases I can find it exciting.

MARCEL DUHAMEL I've never tried it. But I've been tempted to try it, except that I feel it would make me lose my erection.

ANDRÉ BRETON Personally, the idea appalls me, but I can understand how it can be a cause of excitement for others, just like all kinds of preposterous things, peacock feathers, etc.

An imbecile recently claimed that in sexual terms one could categorise women into three types: clitorals, vaginals, uterines. Let us accept this distinction. What percentage of women has Duhamel known in each of the categories?

MARCEL DUHAMEL I've never thought of making such a distinction.

ANDRÉ BRETON Clitorals. It is well known that there are a very few (very, very few) pure clitorals. 5 per cent. The clitoral vaginal-uterines (normal) represent 60 per cent. The vaginals 30 per cent, the uterines 5 per cent.

JEAN CAUPENNE I'm loath to make such a distinction. There are a lot more clitorals.

MARCEL NOLL Yes.

ANDRÉ BRETON Do you know where the clitoris is?

JEAN CAUPENNE The very high percentage of women who do not have orgasms must derive from the fact that they have only normal sexual relations, in which the clitoris is neglected. Thus the number of clitorals would be much higher since many women only come when the mouth is used on the clitoris.

ANDRÉ BRETON I believe that it is very rare for women to have orgasms through the use of the lips and tongue on the clitoris. It's a very uncertain method unless other techniques are also used.

JEAN BALDENSPERGER This kind of view of stimulation of the clitoris as all-powerful tends to make all women into lesbians. (2) All the aids to female masturbation which have been invented have been made for vaginals not clitorals.

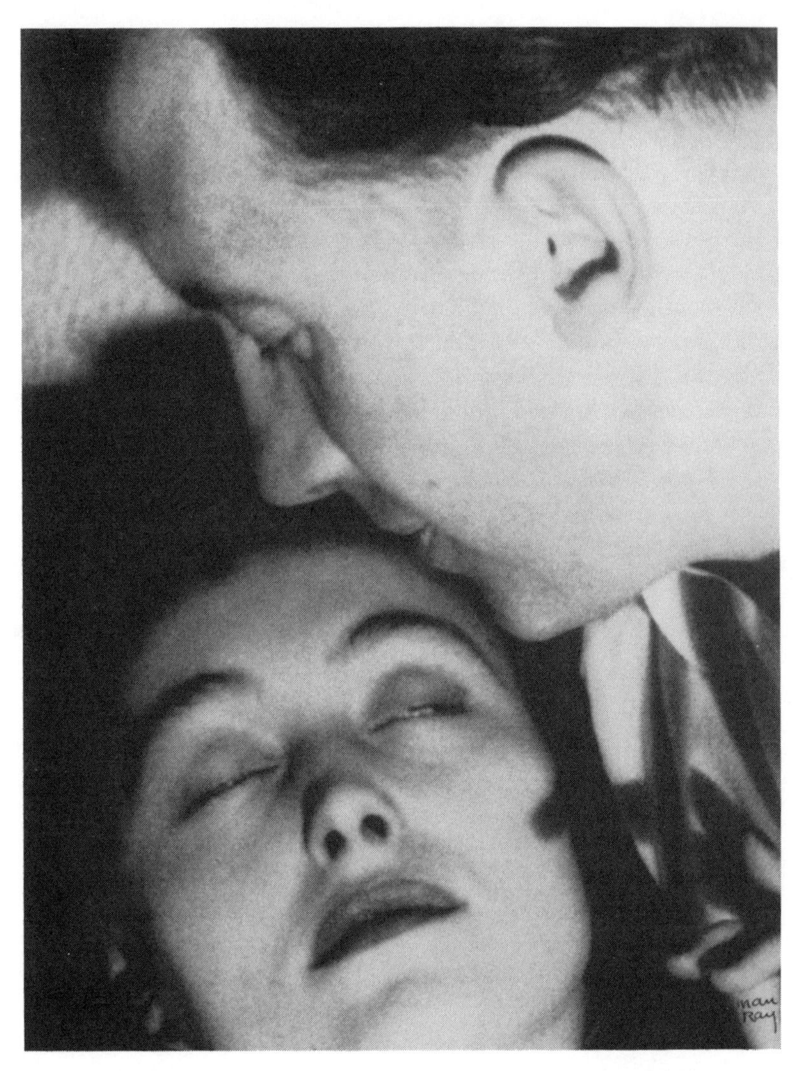

Nusch and Paul Eluard, 1935. Photograph by Man Ray.

Eighth Session

EARLY NOVEMBER 1930

André Breton

Nusch (Eluard)

Paul Eluard

Jeannette Tanguy

Yves Tanguy

André Thirion

Pierre Unik

Madame Unik

Albert Valentin

Simone Vion

(1) What representations accompany desire? In the presence of a woman? Alone? Do certain images [always come to mind]?[1]

PAUL ELUARD What a question! Give me some paper and I'll fill three pages.

Protests from André Breton.

If we're going to insult each other, I won't take part in this discussion. My answer was perfectly reasonable given the question, which is meaningless.

YVES TANGUY There's never any particular image.

ALBERT VALENTIN The most direct images. More direct images take the place of more nebulous ones.

ANDRÉ BRETON If this was a play, I'd be booing Valentin's response. I withdraw my objections. On reflection, I'm rather embarrassed by them.

MADAME UNIK I don't think you can ask the same question of women. In any case, the images are not physical ones.

JEANNETTE TANGUY I have an image . . . (*She is asked to describe it.*) It comes down to a physical impression: someone blond, slim, different from me.

PIERRE UNIK I can't recall any image at the moment.

NUSCH The most direct.

ANDRÉ THIRION When I'm alone, very specific images drawn from a woman I've already slept with or wanted to sleep with. Someone fully clothed, who says nothing. In the presence of a woman, it's completely indefinable, has absolutely no relation to what has provoked desire, to its considered cause. And this cause has no relation to what I can feel on seeing this woman. If I love her, I no longer know anything, it's something infantile, desire on all sides, everywhere.

(2) André Breton, what explicit sexual image do you prefer?

ANDRÉ BRETON The breasts.

YVES TANGUY The buttocks.

JEANNETTE TANGUY The eyes.

ALBERT VALENTIN The arse.

NUSCH The eyes.

PIERRE UNIK The eyes.

André Breton applauds the answers of Tanguy and Valentin and objects strongly to those of Nusch and Unik. The eyes are not sexual.

PAUL ELUARD The sex.

ANDRÉ THIRION A slightly moist cunt. In addition, a very low-cut dress.

JEANNETTE TANGUY The eyes.

(3) Do you like to see the sex? In other words, how do you look at it?

ALBERT VALENTIN I have the very strongest desire to see it.

ANDRÉ BRETON This tells us nothing. The question is badly formulated.

PAUL ELUARD Do you enjoy looking at the sex? In what way? Yours as well as your partners? And in what circumstances?

ANDRÉ BRETON, ANDRÉ THIRION, PAUL ELUARD Very interesting.

ALBERT VALENTIN If it's a woman I love or to whom I'm attached, I like to see her sex, in the most vulnerable positions.

JEANNETTE TANGUY It's not crucial.

NUSCH If it moves, I like to see it. I like to see my own after coitus.

YVES TANGUY In one particular position: the woman on all fours.

PIERRE UNIK My own, never.

YVES TANGUY Damn it, I'd forgotten mine. (*Laughter.*) I like best to see it when I'm alone, with an erection.

JEANNETTE TANGUY We are all great masturbators.

PIERRE UNIK I don't like to see the woman's sex at the start of lovemaking, but when we've been making love for some time the desire to see it can be very strong.

ANDRÉ THIRION I prefer to see the sex in the position described by Tanguy. When I'm making love, vision become complex, it's replaced by touch. As to my own sex, my interest in it comes and goes.

PAUL ELUARD I only like to see my partner's sex when she's masturbating, or masturbating me. I'm sorry. I only like to see my own sex when it's not erect.

ALBERT VALENTIN At least you have plenty of opportunities.

SIMONE VION I don't like to see it at all. I'm afraid of it, I cannot bear to see the man except when he's completely unaroused. As to my own, I never think of it.

ANDRÉ BRETON I couldn't be more in favour of mutual exhibitionism, although I rarely practise it. It must also be said that if I love a woman the question of seeing her sex and *showing* her mine is truly scandalous.

PAUL ELUARD This is an investigation of sexuality, not love.

ANDRÉ BRETON For me there is no 'partner' when I love a woman. We make love when we please.

JEANNETTE TANGUY Very good.

ANDRÉ BRETON I am obliged to make the distinction.

(4) Do you think of seeing your partner's sex when you make love?

YVES TANGUY No, no.

JEANNETTE TANGUY Yes and no. It's something spontaneous.

ALBERT VALENTIN Yes, yes, yes. I'll answer in a moment.

PIERRE UNIK No.

ANDRÉ BRETON The same qualification as before.

NUSCH Yes.

ANDRÉ THIRION When you're making love, sight plays no part.

PAUL ELUARD No, never.

SIMONE VION I feel I'm changing to such an extent that I no longer have any clear ideas about sexuality.

Various objections.

(5) Do you prefer to make love in the daytime (darkness) or at night (light)?

ANDRÉ THIRION Not in the dark.

NUSCH In the light.

SIMONE VION I always have my eyes closed.

JEANNETTE TANGUY I agree with Madame.

ALBERT VALENTIN Preferably in the light. But also at night.

ANDRÉ BRETON If I don't love her, then first in the light then in the dark. If I love her, then in the light by day and in the dark by night.

PAUL ELUARD If everyone answered like Breton, this would become an investigation into the relation between sexuality and love. On all these questions I refuse to answer if we are discussing love.

ANDRÉ THIRION I suggest we leave people free to answer the questions as they understand them and without forcing them to make up their minds on this issue.

ANDRÉ BRETON When I make love to a woman who attracts me, I cannot do so in the dark by day or in the light by night.

PAUL ELUARD Sensuality is something pure in which particular human beings cannot be taken into account.

ANDRÉ BRETON For me, it is impure.

ANDRÉ THIRION I agree.

ANDRÉ BRETON Having taken note of Eluard's objections, we can interpret his responses on the basis of these objections. The only thing that interests me is to make love with someone I love. We've joked around quite enough on this subject, and I have already said that I could go for ten years without making love.

PAUL ELUARD Unik, I hand over to you.

PIERRE UNIK Tanguy, do you imagine something erotic when you first see a woman?

YVES TANGUY Something very precise – caressing her thighs or buttocks.

PAUL ELUARD Never.

ANDRÉ THIRION Always. I imagine a little scenario, in which particular parts of the woman's body, preferably her neck and décolleté, connect with different parts of my own body. Especially the sexual parts.

ALBERT VALENTIN I see a woman, I meet her. Can I love her? If I can, then physical images come into play. If I don't think I can love her, I create an image: of making love with her, of her sex.

NUSCH No.

ANDRÉ BRETON Never a concrete image. Ideas without any organic result. I have never slept with a woman whom I did not believe I could love. Naturally, I have often been mistaken.

NUSCH I'd like to change my answer: I like the mouth rather than the eyes, though the eyes always appeal to me very much.

JEANNETTE TANGUY Eluard was right. Women confuse love and sexuality.

PIERRE UNIK It's very rarely happened to me . . . .

ANDRÉ BRETON Is this a little speech?

PIERRE UNIK No, I can only think of two or three episodes [with women] in my life. I saw them walking in front of me (in other words, only seeing them from behind) and didn't speak to them. Apart from that, never.

ALBERT VALENTIN At least it's a way of distinguishing between women we meet in a café, in the street, in a restaurant.

SIMONE VION If we're going to talk like this, I refuse to speak. I won't accept that.

PAUL ELUARD, YVES TANGUY, ANDRÉ BRETON Prudishness has to intervene every now and then.

SIMONE VION It is not a matter of prudishness.

PIERRE UNIK What do you think of the idea of part of your body coming into contact with that of a woman or a man in a public place or on public transport, with someone you don't know and will never know?

ANDRÉ BRETON If I don't love anyone, it's very good. If I love someone it would never happen.

YVES TANGUY Not interested, whatever the circumstances.

JEANNETTE TANGUY It cannot be a good thing.

ANDRÉ THIRION As long as I don't find her physically unattractive, and she's not too skinny, I always enjoy it.

SIMONE VION It's all I can do not to make this a question of prudishness again.

PAUL ELUARD In the dark, if I'm able to imagine someone, I can indulge in it. In the daylight, it always makes me sad, even if the woman is very pretty.

ANDRÉ BRETON It does not happen very often.

ALBERT VALENTIN It's a question of whether I or the other person makes the contact. But either way it always appeals to me.

NUSCH It disgusts me.

SIMONE VION I'd like to add something. In the dark I think it's always pleasant.

ALBERT VALENTIN At last, after a whole hour, a human voice is heard.

Approval.

PAUL ELUARD I'd like a woman to ask a question.

Approval.

NUSCH How do you like to make love?

ALBERT VALENTIN You mean one sex inserted into another?

PAUL ELUARD As you know very well, to make love means to ejaculate.

ALBERT VALENTIN What does making love mean?

Confused interruptions.

ANDRÉ THIRION At present, I love someone: no a priori representation. At other times, I had preferences.

YVES TANGUY I can make love in every way. I prefer sodomy.

NUSCH Sitting astride the man.

JEANNETTE TANGUY On my own.

SIMONE VION I'm not going to answer. I don't attach any great importance to it, especially at the beginning of a relationship.

ANDRÉ BRETON Taking everything into account, it is sodomy which seems to me to have the greatest possibilities, although I don't like it.

PAUL ELUARD All positions where the woman is active.

ANDRÉ BRETON That's just laziness.

PAUL ELUARD What kind of caress do you prefer? One that's both active and passive?

ANDRÉ BRETON I cannot entirely accept either the word 'caress' or that question.

PAUL ELUARD What do you most like to touch, to caress, be it with the mouth or the hands?

ANDRÉ THIRION I prefer to caress the woman's sex. Or for her to unbutton my flies and take my cock in her hand.

NUSCH To stroke a man's sex. For him to stroke my breasts.

ANDRÉ BRETON I don't like anyone to caress me. I hate that. I like to stroke women's stomachs.

SIMONE VION I don't like that at all. I like hair in general.

YVES TANGUY Very rarely. Sometimes the balls. As to the caresses that I give, the hair and the top of the thighs with my arm.

JEANNETTE TANGUY I can only explain with gestures. Along all the joins and folds of the body.

PAUL ELUARD I like to stroke the neck, the breasts and the armpits. I only like my breasts to be stroked.

ALBERT VALENTIN I like to caress the armpits and the hollow of the hips.

ANDRÉ BRETON Always the joker, aren't you?

ALBERT VALENTIN The sex and the buttocks. I like my sex being caressed.

(6) How many times have you been able to come consecutively, without leaving the room?

YVES TANGUY Six times (between ten in the evening and eleven in the morning, when I was twenty-two).

ANDRÉ THIRION Four times (in one night, at twenty-two).

ANDRÉ BRETON Four or five times (at thirty-two, in the space of fourteen hours).

NUSCH Five times (between midnight and eleven in the morning, at twenty-three-and-a-half).

ALBERT VALENTIN Twice (in one night, at twenty-seven).

ANDRÉ BRETON I admire Valentin's answer, if he's not joking.

PIERRE UNIK Five times (between eleven at night and ten in the morning, at nineteen).

JEANNETTE TANGUY Four times (between nine and eleven years old, between nine o'clock and eleven o'clock).

PAUL ELUARD I'm ashamed. Eleven times.

You're going to laugh at me again. I'm thirty-five. Which should make you think. Eleven times in normal circumstances. Seven times with a woman who had her period. Eleven times when I was twenty between nine in the evening and one in the afternoon.

ANDRÉ BRETON I'd like to come back to my initial question. I would like to know what a man does when he thinks the woman has come, or hasn't come.

ANDRÉ THIRION In the best circumstances (with someone I particularly like) I can go on until the woman comes.

YVES TANGUY I can't think of anything more annoying.

ANDRÉ BRETON Can you carry on?

YVES TANGUY A few times I have.

PIERRE UNIK I'm at a loss to know what to do. I've always had the impression that women came before I did.

ANDRÉ BRETON Why are you at a loss? Is the impediment[2] mental or physical?

PIERRE UNIK It has always seemed impossible to me. To go on, that is.

ANDRÉ BRETON It fills me with despair, but I see no solution to the problem.

PAUL ELUARD I entirely approve of Unik's optimism.

ANDRÉ BRETON And I disapprove of it.

PAUL ELUARD At present, at any rate, I can delay my orgasm long enough to feel that I respond to the woman's inevitable signs of pleasure. My pessimism has never allowed me to imagine complete openness in sexual relations. When I was young I could also continue to be active after coming. Now that's almost impossible, but in consequence I take much longer to reach orgasm than I did then, and – despite my pessimism – I have never had the slightest inclination to imagine that the woman who showed me she was satisfied had not in fact had an orgasm.

ANDRÉ BRETON As far as I'm concerned, my optimism on sexual matters does not stop me thinking that the signs of passion you refer to are not only not inevitable but, insofar as they correspond to a reality, can be equivocal. Even when I was younger, I was never able to continue sexual activity without any ill effects after reaching orgasm. In the end I accepted that it was beyond me. If I tried, the result would be the sort of physical discomfort in the abdomen in face of which I refuse to imagine anything whatsoever.

ANDRÉ THIRION I am unable to make love with someone I think is faking.

ANDRÉ BRETON To my mind, it is not a question of the woman faking. Just now someone rightly said that the woman's orgasm was more diffuse, less concentrated in time. From my reading, I believe that the woman (because the man only comes when he ejaculates) is in a state which is a little less intense and more prolonged . . .

SIMONE VION There is a state of heightening pleasure, and there is the state of orgasm.

ANDRÉ BRETON Even though we know that orgasm is a limit for us, how can we be sure that it is the same for the woman?

SIMONE VION Personally, I think that when orgasm is over, I want to stop.

PAUL ELUARD Not all women think . . . .

ANDRÉ BRETON If a man has ten women (a harem), he can come with the first, and come with the second, but not with the tenth. On the other hand, a woman can carry on one after the other.

JEANNETTE TANGUY No.

PAUL ELUARD They have polyandry in Tibet.

NUSCH Better and better. The more she has, the more she wants. (If I love.)

YVES TANGUY I think it's very frequent.

PAUL ELUARD I slept with another man and a woman. This woman who was more excited than the two men (judging by appearances), aroused the two of them and made love with both of them. She had no reason to pretend.

ANDRÉ BRETON She was pretending.

SIMONE VION Did she come? She couldn't tell.

ANDRÉ BRETON If we're talking about pleasure, I agree. I could pretend with women, enjoy myself with several women without coming.

PAUL ELUARD I am incapable of pretending.

ANDRÉ BRETON I recently saw a woman using a little rubber bulb to squirt liquid into her sex. It was really rather touching.

PAUL ELUARD It's rather like the real thing. I've often tried to fake it, I've never succeeded. I've stayed awake, or barely sleeping, for nights on end, but in the end fatigue wins out.

ANDRÉ BRETON If I desire a woman, it makes no difference to me whether she comes or not.

ANDRÉ THIRION I disagree entirely, I especially want her to come.

YVES TANGUY I agree.

PAUL ELUARD Sadness prevents me starting again. The impediment isn't physical but mental with a woman one does not love. The whole problem of pessimism is contained there: from the pessimism which follows the act of love to the more general pessimism about no longer being joined together, etc.

ANDRÉ BRETON In one of Boccaccio's stories, which I read before I had any experience of love, a man goes to sleep still inside a woman. That's something really crazy.

PIERRE UNIK Not at all.

PAUL ELUARD, ANDRÉ THIRION It's really mad.

ANDRÉ BRETON If the same thing happened to me, I'd kill myself when I woke up.

PAUL ELUARD But it can happen that when you're making love with a woman you desire very much, you stay aroused throughout the night. But still sleep. So Boccaccio's story is possible.

ANDRÉ BRETON No. The mind is dead. So it's a simulacrum, because it's the continuation of something which no longer exists.

PAUL ELUARD I've slept through the night holding a woman and remaining aroused.

ANDRÉ THIRION That is possible.

ANDRÉ BRETON I detach myself from the woman. We know that we move around in all sorts of ways during the night. One can test it out: which kinds of contacts during sleep cause one to wake up.

PAUL ELUARD Nothing matters more to a man than his sleep.

ANDRÉ BRETON The person who can fall asleep making love doesn't exist.

PAUL ELUARD I've woken up making love with the person I went to bed with. I stopped.

ANDRÉ THIRION Something similar happened to me, The person was asleep. I tried to make love with her, she responded: after a moment she woke up. I'm not absolutely sure that she was not asleep.

YVES TANGUY Doesn't fatigue arouse your sexual capacity?

ANDRÉ BRETON The question is not very well put.

André Thirion (standing) and Georges Sadoul, on a walking holiday in the Hautes-Vosges, 1926. (Collection André Thirion)

Ninth Session

24 NOVEMBER 1930

Bauer[1]

Pierre Blum

André Breton

Paul Eluard

Humm

Madame Léna

Victor Mayer

Raymond Michelet

Schnitzler

Schwartz

André Thirion

Katia Thirion

Pierre Unik

Albert Valentin

Simone Vion

ANDRÉ THIRION How many times have you made love – the maximum – without leaving the room?

HUMM Four times.

ANDRÉ BRETON I would like additional information on age.

HUMM Twenty-seven (I'm twenty-eight). The woman was twenty-six or twenty-seven.

SCHNITZLER Six times at twenty-one (I'm twenty-seven). The woman was seventeen.

MADAME LÉNA It's a little complicated!

ANDRÉ THIRION I'm not asking for absolute precision.

MADAME LÉNA At eighteen? At no matter what age (at fifteen or at twenty). The man was thirty-eight.

SCHWARTZ Three times (at twenty-five). I'm twenty-five. The woman was twenty-five.

PIERRE BLUM Seven times (at twenty-two and a half). I'm twenty-three. The woman was twenty-seven.

ANDRÉ BRETON Four or five times (at thirty-two). I'm thirty-four. The woman was thirty.

ALBERT VALENTIN Twice. The woman was twenty-six.

RAYMOND MICHELET Twice (at eighteen). I'm eighteen. The woman was twenty.

VICTOR MAYER Eleven times at twenty-three. The woman was seventeen.

PAUL ELUARD Eleven times at twenty. The woman was twenty-five.

SIMONE VION Three times at twenty-two. The man was twenty-five.

PIERRE UNIK Five times at nineteen. The woman was twenty-four.

KATIA THIRION Three times at twenty-three. The man was twenty-two.

ANDRÉ THIRION Five times at twenty-two. I am twenty-three. The woman was forty or forty-two.

PAUL ELUARD What proportion has there been of impotence, in which you have not been able to make love even though you intended to?

ANDRÉ THIRION I don't understand the question. I've experienced episodes of impotence. I can recall three or four. But I can't give a proportion. One of these episodes happened with the woman I was talking about earlier. In '28 or '29 I went through a period of sexual depression following the departure of Katia. The impotence occurred with the first woman with whom I had the opportunity to make love, as a result of this depression. On the second occasion I think it was caused by sexual melancholy, and depression.

KATIA THIRION It has happened to me once. I wanted to make love and I couldn't. I kept seeing someone else instead of the person who was there.

PIERRE UNIK I've never been unable to make love at least once. But I've quite often been unable to make love more than once.

ANDRÉ BRETON Why? Because you were satiated?

PIERRE UNIK Often enough, yes.

ANDRÉ BRETON Was this psychic or organic?

PIERRE UNIK It's difficult to define, for it's hard to separate the two. In the majority of cases it was psychic. But perhaps it was organic and I didn't want to admit it. I would always debate it, but I'm not sure how accurate my conclusions were.

SIMONE VION I will reply in a minute.

PAUL ELUARD Until I was twenty-five, never. Later, often. The reason: almost always because of my ignorance of the woman. Physical ignorance. If I can make love with her once, I can start again. (2) Often because I didn't know the woman well enough. (3) Because her great beauty led me to admire her platonically. (4) Alcohol and tobacco: complete incapacity. (5) Absence of desire. (6) Desire for solitude caused both by the presence of the woman and by the wish to be alone.

VICTOR MAYER Never.

RAYMOND MICHELET Around the age of seventeen, it happened to me for physical reasons (nervous tension). From eighteen onwards it has often happened because I was dissatisfied. And this dissatisfaction begins before the woman is completely undressed, and my inability to perform increases as she gets undressed.

ALBERT VALENTIN Never.

ANDRÉ BRETON It has only happened to me once – after an exhausting journey with a woman I desired who was not yet my mistress. But even when I was very young, I always felt anxious at the thought of making love with a woman I desired. Since then, I've been absolutely unable to conceive of making love with a woman I merely desired.

PAUL ELUARD I'd like Breton to elaborate on the first part of his answer.

ANDRÉ BRETON I attributed this impotence to the mauve wallpaper in the room – I've always found the colour mauve particularly unbearable.

PIERRE BLUM Yes – because of nervous tension caused by timidity or inexperience – or because of the presence of a third person.

ANDRÉ BRETON I'd like to add that I'm convinced that in my case the desire to begin again precedes the ability to begin again successfully.

PAUL ELUARD I would add that after my first experience of impotence, I dreaded the idea that it would happen again – which made it happen again with other women.

SCHWARTZ (1) When I made love the first time, from fear of not succeeding. The woman was thirty-seven. (2) The second attempt, with the same woman, the next day, without success. (3) I don't know what to attribute it to – for fear of impotence wasn't there: I'd already proved my virility. (4) Total lack of desire – because of depression, of solitude preceding or of a longing simply for tenderness. (5) Physical repulsion because of the age of a whore. She was between fifty and seventy years old.

MADAME LÉNA Whether through love, friendship or vice, I've always been satisfied.

SCHNITZLER Until I was twenty-one, it never happened. At twenty-one I encountered a woman who was physically very dirty: this affected me strongly and made me impotent. This impotence recurs quite regularly, almost every year, when I think of that woman. Every time I do, I am absolutely unable to perform.

HUMM The first time I made love – I was nineteen – I experienced complete impotence because of repulsion and nervous tension. Later it happened with a woman I liked very much. I felt intellectually inferior to her, and that feeling produced the impotence. It has never happened since, except with a girl who excited me but when I went to bed with her I was completely impotent because of fatigue (resulting from walking in the mountains). Also, the fear of pregnancy and the woman's resistance.

SIMONE VION I reserve my answer. I don't want to answer in these circumstances.

ANDRÉ BRETON How many people have you made love with? Approximately?

HUMM Very difficult. I would guess around one hundred.

SCHNITZLER Fifty or so.

MADAME LÉNA One hundred and fifty.

SCHWARTZ About ten.

PIERRE BLUM Four.

ANDRÉ BRETON Thirty-five.

ALBERT VALENTIN Three or four hundred.

RAYMOND MICHELET Six or seven.

VICTOR MAYER Several hundred. I can't remember – maybe a hundred women in four weeks.

PAUL ELUARD Between five hundred and one thousand. I could work it out more or less precisely.

SIMONE VION Between fifteen and twenty. Closer to twenty.

PIERRE UNIK Between fifteen and twenty.

KATIA THIRION Three.

ANDRÉ THIRION Thirty-five to sixty.

HUMM I would like to ask what is your longest period of abstinence – the longest time without making love.

PAUL ELUARD Without having intercourse?

HUMM Simply without having sexual relations with a woman.

ANDRÉ THIRION The longest period of abstinence you've known, even though you could have made love during this time.

PAUL ELUARD Do we count prostitutes?

ANDRÉ THIRION Five months, during which I tried but without success. I formed relationships with women in order to sleep with them. I didn't succeed.

PAUL ELUARD *Is that voluntary abstinence?* That is all we are concerned with. Abstinence means refusal: going without: denying yourself something.

ANDRÉ BRETON I can be continent for two years.

ANDRÉ THIRION Let me go on. Apart from that, I didn't try for a month and a half, but during that time I masturbated. I can't go longer than four days without masturbating or making love.

KATIA THIRION Eighteen months without making love. Without caressing myself or anything.

PIERRE UNIK I went for nine or ten months without making love. I masturbated during that time. I can go for a month or three weeks without masturbating. After a great emotional trauma I can go for two months without even thinking about masturbating.

SIMONE VION I can go without it for several months. I think this is changing.

PAUL ELUARD I'm in a bad way if I go for a week without making love. Not a day passes without sexual desire. I can go for a week without masturbating, or very rarely doing it: ten times a year, on average. Less and less.

SIMONE VION When I start again after this time, I feel that I could go without.

VICTOR MAYER One week maximum. After a week, I'm almost crazy. I don't masturbate more than ten times a year.

RAYMOND MICHELET I've gone for almost five months without making love. During that time, frequent masturbation – minimum of once a week. And some of the time, masturbation several times a day.

ALBERT VALENTIN No more than forty-eight hours without making love with a woman I love or with prostitutes. If I haven't got any money, I masturbate.

ANDRÉ BRETON I've twice spent two years without making love – now, masturbation is more frequent (three times in four days). Impossible to sleep with a woman I don't love or think I love.

PIERRE BLUM Two or two and a half months, masturbating every week. Currently, eight to ten days.

SCHWARTZ For a period of nine months with masturbation becoming more and more frequent (one every two days). Currently, three weeks.

MADAME LÉNA Two years without making love following a great sorrow. Currently, one week maximum, during which I often give myself pleasure.

SCHNITZLER Six months with masturbation at least once or several times a week.

HUMM A year and a half without making love. Masturbation every three weeks. Then three months without doing anything.

What do you think about when you masturbate?[2]

ANDRÉ THIRION When I masturbate I picture several scenes: different women with whom, for example, I haven't slept but whom I have strongly desired. I imagine these people displaying certain (erotic) parts of their bodies. In two other cases, I imagined a woman I loved. The way I get erections has evolved. At seventeen I would think of a particular person while I masturbated. Currently, there's a whole series of images linked after the fashion of a dream. I always come.

ALBERT VALENTIN At first I think of a woman I loved, sucking me. During masturbation the image changes to other, less identifiable women. At the moment of orgasm I go back to the first image. I always come.

PAUL ELUARD I usually think of a woman I've loved, my wife,[3] and usually I imagine her making love with me or in general (for pleasure). I enjoy looking at my sex. Sometimes I don't come. Usually I come. When I don't come it's because of some particularly degrading idea, and from the desire to go off and make love with a woman. This answer is self-interested and entirely untrue.

ANDRÉ BRETON It is accompanied by a series of fleeting images of different women (dream women I knew or know but never a woman I have loved). As a general rule, I stop at ejaculation.

KATIA THIRION I prefer to answer last.

PIERRE UNIK I started masturbating at thirteen. First stage: no female image. Second stage: imaginary images following a first contact (after a certain number of encounters). Third stage: images relating to real experiences. Never any images of intercourse. Main preoccupation: the woman's response. Very often I don't ejaculate for fear of feeling depressed afterwards.

VICTOR MAYER Between six and eleven (before first contact with a woman), very vague and speculative images of the sexual act (fragmentary). Afterwards I never thought about a woman I was sleeping with. Until sixteen I had images of genital sexuality; then oral sexuality.

SCHWARTZ Never any precise images of women but the woman's sex always plays a part without being truly pictured. It's a very fleeting thing. Currently, the sight of my own sex. I always come and I never think of a woman I've loved. Currently my images tend to be tactile or erotic.

PIERRE BLUM Three stages: (1) Before the first sexual relationship. (2) Having had relations without love, image of an imaginary person. (3) Having loved: I never imagine the person loved. In these images I identify with the people I imagine. I avoid ejaculation one time out of every three.

SCHNITZLER Two very different kinds. Very often images of people I haven't been able to have. Images of many erotic scenes with lots of people (orgies), for example, at a beach or swimming-pool. Very often displays of tenderness where touch plays a part.

MADAME LÉNA When I masturbate I enjoy it right to the end, thinking of a woman I loved very much – my sister.

HUMM Two periods. From fifteen to seventeen: when I hadn't known a woman – except platonically. From seventeen to nineteen: narcissistic images like those of Schwartz. Then, having known a woman, from nineteen to twenty-five, sadistic images where the woman was always the victim. Since then I have always avoided love with imaginary women.

KATIA THIRION During my childhood, two sexes: the man's and the woman's. The idea of love was very vague. Having made love, never any images – except a dream: the man's sex moving, and I never succeed in coming as I do when I make love. I even feel disgust.

RAYMOND MICHELET Always orgasm. Before having sexual relations, no images.

Subsequently the images came late – at the point of ejaculation. It's an unconscious state, like a dream: female images, never more than two or three, no one I really know, except from chance encounters, images that here returned in dreams.

SIMONE VION I only do it when I'm reading. Then comes orgasm. I started quite a long time after first making love with a man. Now it's mechanical and happens quite fast. Whatever happens, I don't picture anything. I feel a kind of unconsciousness. I've sometimes picked up a book – never an erotic one – in order to do it.

PAUL ELUARD Have you ever masturbated to ejaculation in front of someone of the opposite sex without hiding it?

HUMM Yes, once.

SCHNITZLER Very often.

MADAME LÉNA Very often.

PIERRE BLUM Never. I find the idea unacceptable.

SCHWARTZ Twice. Once in the dark.

ALBERT VALENTIN Almost always.

VICTOR MAYER Very often.

PAUL ELUARD Very often.

SIMONE VION Never. And it will be a long time before I do. An intolerable idea.

PIERRE UNIK Many times, with one woman only.

RAYMOND MICHELET Never. No particular wish to.

KATIA THIRION Never. But I don't find the idea intolerable.

ANDRÉ THIRION Twice. Once, in spite of my objections. It was really awful. The second time too.

ANDRÉ BRETON A few times. With only one woman, whom I didn't love.

ANDRÉ THIRION Do you touch yourself before or after making love?

General 'yes', except Simone Vion, Schwartz, André Thirion.

HUMM Since puberty have you felt a conscious attraction to someone of the same sex, and how often?

VICTOR MAYER Yes. Not often. Two or three times in my life.

PAUL ELUARD Never. No, wait, once, when I was very young.

SIMONE VION For many women, beginning with the feeling that the woman loved me. Unrequited love for a girl I loved, platonic love.

ALBERT VALENTIN Never, never.

RAYMOND MICHELET Perhaps once, in a very vague way.

KATIA THIRION Never.

ANDRÉ THIRION Once very definitely, at seventeen, for a boy of thirteen.

ANDRÉ BRETON Never.

HUMM After the age of fifteen, never.

MADAME LÉNA Very often, with many women.

SCHNITZLER Three times.

PIERRE BLUM Once.

SCHWARTZ Never.

PIERRE UNIK No.

ALBERT VALENTIN To what extent are the women interested in sexual relations between two men, and how much do they think about it? How favourably do they look on this and how do they imagine such relations? Also, are they in favour of relations between two women, and have they ever experienced them?

KATIA THIRION Between two men, the idea totally disgusts me. I try not to imagine such relations. Between two women I can just about accept it; I've never done it.

MADAME LÉNA Between men I accept it without any problem at all, and I find the thought very exciting. I like the idea of two men caressing each other, on the sex for example, but not having anal intercourse. I have a very strong desire to see it. I accept it without any problem between women as well, I am entirely in favour of such relationships. I have had sixteen women.

SIMONE VION I don't feel the slightest disgust for it. I've had very good friends who were homosexuals and the idea doesn't disturb me. Indifference. No images. I've literally turned down several women because I didn't desire them, but it's bound to happen, quite soon. I've never done it.

Same question put to the men.

SCHWARTZ Between two women I don't see any problem, it excites me very slightly, not in any precise way. Between two men, it leaves me cold. I haven't done it yet. A degree of disgust.

PIERRE BLUM Between two women, I can very easily accept it. Between two men it doesn't shock me, but I don't like effeminate men. Never done it.

SCHNITZLER I accept everything. For me it's the same act, the same thing. I've done it three times.

HUMM I cannot think of relations between men without disgust. Between women I don't like it at all, but it doesn't really disgust me. Never done it!

ANDRÉ THIRION In theory, relations between women please me, in practice I find them repellent. Between men, in practice I find it impossible, though I've tried, without any result.

RAYMOND MICHELET Same thing as Thirion.

ALBERT VALENTIN Very much in favour of relations between women. I like to join in, even with the woman I love. Homosexuals, be they amateur or professional, disgust me more than anything in the world. Never done it.

PAUL ELUARD The greatest hatred for 'male' lesbians, the greatest weakness for lesbians who remain women. I abhor relations between men, because of the mental deformity they produce. Never done it!

VICTOR MAYER I loathe lesbians who want to play a male role, the others excite me. Relations between men disgust me, I find it ridiculous, as ludicrous as sex between a star and a dog. Never done it.

ANDRÉ BRETON Same answer as Valentin. I find lesbians very appealing.

PIERRE UNIK Relations between women used to greatly excite me and now excite me much less. But I look on them favourably. Physically, relations between men absolutely disgust me.

How do you imagine relations between two women and between two men?

BAUER Between two women, circular erotic relations. Between two men I refuse to imagine it in any way at all. Homosexuality is something that isolates the individual totally from the social group.

PAUL ELUARD In every way: oral, masturbatory, etc. Between men: I can imagine. I've read books. It doesn't interest me.

PIERRE UNIK Between women: mutual masturbation and kissing. Between men: I never imagine anything. It's of no interest.

SIMONE VION Never any image of it.

RAYMOND MICHELET Between women: masturbation, kisses. Between men: no single dominant image.

KATIA THIRION Between men: I imagine all that they can do. It doesn't interest me. Between women: cunnilingus. And that doesn't interest me either.

ANDRÉ THIRION Women: caressing the breasts. For men, no image.

PIERRE BLUM Women: succubi. For men, I don't think about it.

HUMM For women: tenderness, caresses – going as far as cunnilingus. Men: no image.

MADAME LÉNA Men caressing each other. Women: sex on sex.

SCHNITZLER Men: masturbation. Women: masturbation and caresses.

SCHWARTZ Women: caresses over the whole body and sex on sex. With men: caresses over the whole body.

ANDRÉ BRETON For women: oral-erotic relations. For men: unrestrained sodomy. I find the whole thing utterly repugnant – active or passive, they're all fucked.

ALBERT VALENTIN For men: disgust prevents me imagining anything. For women: strictly oral (mouth on sex) and only in so far as I can join in.

MADAME LÉNA At what age did you first (1) ejaculate and (2) make love?

PIERRE UNIK (1) Thirteen. (2) Sixteen.

PAUL ELUARD (1) Thirteen. (2) Fourteen and a half.
SIMONE VION Sixteen.
RAYMOND MICHELET (1) Twelve. (2) Seventeen.
ANDRÉ BRETON (1) Thirteen. (2) Eighteen.
KATIA THIRION (1) Eight. (2) Twenty.
ANDRÉ THIRION (1) Eleven. (2) Sixteen.
HUMM (1) Thirteen. (2) Nineteen.
VICTOR MAYER (1) Nine. (2) Twelve.
PIERRE BLUM (1) Fourteen. (2) Twenty-two.
MADAME LÉNA (1) Eight. (2) Eleven.
SCHNITZLER (1) Fifteen. (2) Eighteen.
SCHWARTZ Twenty-two.
ALBERT VALENTIN (1) Eleven. (2) Sixteen.

What do you say at the moment of climax?

PIERRE UNIK The most I've said was: 'Ah!'
SIMONE VION I don't say anything.
RAYMOND MICHELET Nothing.
ANDRÉ BRETON Nothing.
ANDRÉ THIRION I think I once said: 'Darling.'
HUMM (*Total silence.*)
VICTOR MAYER Nothing.
PIERRE BLUM With the person I love: 'Darling.' Otherwise, nothing.
MADAME LÉNA Normally I say: 'Fernande' (my sister) or maybe: 'Dani' (a doctor I loved a lot, with whom I've never slept), or: 'Pierre'.
SCHNITZLER Nothing.
SCHWARTZ 'My darling' or maybe: 'My baby'.
KATIA THIRION 'I love you (a.o.i . . .)'.[4]
ALBERT VALENTIN 'Slut!', 'Filth!', 'Whore!', etc.
PAUL ELUARD I don't stop talking.

Yves Tanguy. (Collection Madame G. Duhamel)

Tenth Session

26 NOVEMBER 1930

André Breton

Paul Eluard

Jeannette Tanguy

Yves Tanguy

Pierre Unik

PAUL ELUARD Yves, how did you imagine the, how can I put it? . . . the . . . the resumption . . . the . . . the beginning . . . Shit! . . . When you were a child, how did you imagine approaching a woman of a different sex? . . . [1], how did you imagine having amorous relations? By kissing? By caressing? Was it by touching? Was it . . .

YVES TANGUY That's very vague.

PAUL ELUARD Do you see what I mean? You thought of women. In what way?

YVES TANGUY Yes, I see very well, but . . . By less direct things. Conversation, among others. Things that were very remote.

PAUL ELUARD So by their presence, in other words.

YVES TANGUY Precisely.

PAUL ELUARD And Unik?

PIERRE UNIK Difficult.

PAUL ELUARD (*apologises for the second time*) 'I was a child, a virgin, and in love'.

PIERRE UNIK It was all greatly idealized.

PAUL ELUARD But it's always possible to imagine sexual relations. Physical relations. After all, you were fully developed.

PIERRE UNIK I didn't think I'd be able to sleep with her. But I could conceive of the question. Around sixteen.

PAUL ELUARD Not before?

PIERRE UNIK No. Before, I had physical images, I had sexual desires and perhaps very strong ones, but not in relation to a specific woman.

PAUL ELUARD So in relation to images? Naked bodies or heads? Did you see the body in these images?

PIERRE UNIK Very little.

ANDRÉ BRETON The face. This took shape very late (seventeen or eighteen years old) in connection with the paintings of Gustave Moreau (a face, a look). Absolutely ideal love.

PAUL ELUARD You were naturally aware of the possibility of physical relationships?

ANDRÉ BRETON Yes, from about the age of nine, revelations provided by a pupil at elementary school, indissociably linked to images of French history (he did drawings from history), specially to the picture of Charles the Bald, and to a horrible song, *Père Nostrom*.

YVES TANGUY Very strange. There's a dirty story about Charles the

Bald, who used to masturbate every morning (who blew his brains out, etc.).

PAUL ELUARD How did you find out you could masturbate?

ANDRÉ BRETON In Lorient, when I was about twelve, if my memory serves me well, in Breton-style water-closets. On my own. I never heard anyone talk about it. Profoundly pleasurable, but worried about ejaculation.

PAUL ELUARD Unik, did you have any sexual relations accompanied by desires before you masturbated. Did it excite you? Did it worry you?

PIERRE UNIK Well before? No.

PAUL ELUARD Did the idea excite you, arouse any desire?

PIERRE UNIK At eight I knew a little girl. It was absolutely pure. I kissed her on the face.

PAUL ELUARD You never dreamt of looking at a little girl's sex?

PIERRE UNIK No, never, not once.

PAUL ELUARD Had you seen the sex of a grown-up?

PIERRE UNIK Never, not until I made love.

PAUL ELUARD When did you first masturbate?

PIERRE UNIK I learnt about it from a chap called Cordebarre, in school.

PAUL ELUARD He showed you?

PIERRE UNIK He only told me about it. He explained how to do it. I immediately associated it with the word *onanism* which I'd seen in the dictionary, which had struck me because of the baneful disorders that it caused. I saw objections to it, and told him about them.

PAUL ELUARD Concerning health?

PIERRE UNIK Yes. As several other friends spoke to me about it, I tried.

PAUL ELUARD I masturbated, I didn't ejaculate (twelve years old). I masturbated for six months without ejaculation. But with orgasm.

YVES TANGUY I masturbated from the age of five, with orgasm every time. Ejaculation happened around the age of ten or eleven.

PIERRE UNIK This is a very stupid question, never mind. Don't take any notice. But in an utterly absolute sense, do you think it's good to make love? Even if you don't want to?

PAUL ELUARD Is it to be recommended?

PIERRE UNIK Not exactly. Morally, is it a good thing, even without a particular woman in mind? Even without desire?

PAUL ELUARD That's a very good question.

ANDRÉ BRETON Without having an irresistible desire?

YVES TANGUY Why?

ANDRÉ BRETON Without some physical or mental necessity, we're talking about an *acte gratuit*, which I cannot imagine, or a piece of braggadocio.

PAUL ELUARD It's no more conceivable than masturbation without images of women, but nevertheless I insist that, for me, making love is to be recommended. But for me this is a moral idea.

ANDRÉ BRETON Why?

PAUL ELUARD I consider chastity as immoral and harmful.

ANDRÉ BRETON Why?

PAUL ELUARD Because for me sexual preoccupation is the basis of all mental activity.

ANDRÉ BRETON I consider sexual love as something which empties the mind of almost all ideas.

PAUL ELUARD Absolutely opposed, a priori.

YVES TANGUY A priori?

PAUL ELUARD And a posteriori.

ANDRÉ BRETON Why a priori?

PAUL ELUARD Desire gives me as much mental satisfaction as the satisfaction of that desire.

ANDRÉ BRETON Well then! Why satisfy the desire?

PAUL ELUARD To renew it.

ANDRÉ BRETON With one person after another?

PAUL ELUARD Or with the same person, it doesn't make any difference.

ANDRÉ BRETON Why does one renew desire? Is it insufficient in itself, and if one judges that it is, in the last analysis, insufficient in itself, why renew it?

PAUL ELUARD To renew the object of the desire.

ANDRÉ BRETON To renew the object, in such a case, can only be by changing it.

PAUL ELUARD Absolutely, even when the person doesn't change. For me no one realisation of desire corresponds[2] to another.

ANDRÉ BRETON That idea tends to elevate the idea of love over the being whom one loves or wants to love, that is to say, to turn them into a means. I love women too much, and I believe I am too susceptible to loving *a* woman, not to object to such an attitude.

PAUL ELUARD It is not the idea of love which creates a being, but a being in love who, to make life possible, tends to change it (life). Life is only monotonous if one does not love, and the variations of desire and the satisfaction of this desire concern love. One cannot love if desire is always the same.

ANDRÉ BRETON [. . .] [3] Would Tanguy enjoy being sodomised by a woman using a dildo?

YVES TANGUY Very much. Rather a new question for me. No connection with homosexuality!

PAUL ELUARD I've never been buggered, and I could only permit such a thing if I thought it was necessary to the woman I love from an erotic point of view.

PIERRE UNIK The question seems to me to be completely mad.

ANDRÉ BRETON It's a question which I would absolutely uphold on theoretical grounds, since the woman could not derive any physical pleasure from it and nor, I imagine, could the man.

PIERRE UNIK What, then? An intellectual pleasure?

ANDRÉ BRETON An intellectual 'pleasure'.

PIERRE UNIK (*Gesture of incomprehension.*)

PAUL ELUARD (*To Breton.*) Could you, if you loved a woman who was very perverse, give yourself to a man if she desired it?

ANDRÉ BRETON The question would not come up because I would not love such a woman, my taste for perversity in women doesn't go that far.

PAUL ELUARD (*Protests.*) I don't know how you can say that you would not love such a woman, for this desire might well have been born during your love.

ANDRÉ BRETON Love in such a case would have ended long before.

André Breton: *Self-Portrait: L'écriture automatique*, 1938.
(Collection Arturo Schwarz)

Eleventh Session

26 JANUARY 1931

André Breton

Paul Eluard

Georges Sadoul

Pierre Unik

Albert Valentin

PAUL ELUARD Sadoul, have you ever made love between a woman's breasts?

GEORGES SADOUL No. I don't like breasts which are very close together and I find the idea of pushing them together disagreeable.

ALBERT VALENTIN Yes. With two women who were my mistresses.

ANDRÉ BRETON Since men have a cock between two balls, how is it that women have nothing between their breasts?

ALBERT VALENTIN There's no answer to that.

PAUL ELUARD No.

GEORGES SADOUL Er . . . um . . . I refuse to answer that question.

PAUL ELUARD It's raining.

ANDRÉ BRETON Valentin, what would you like to have instead of your cock?

ALBERT VALENTIN . . . This is an investigation of sexuality. So, spunk for sure!

ANDRÉ BRETON Sadoul, what would you like to have instead of air?

GEORGES SADOUL . . . Breathing.

PIERRE UNIK Breton, what's your response when it's said of a woman, 'she's really hot for it'?

ANDRÉ BRETON It's a goatish expression . . .

PAUL ELUARD Breton, do you think Baffo was a pig?[1]

ANDRÉ BRETON That remains to be seen, but Baffo has written at least one admirable poem, perhaps the only one, which is entitled 'Exaggeration on the Theme of a Pussy'.

PAUL ELUARD And what do you think in general of erotic literature, by which I mean literature which gives a name to what it's talking about?

ANDRÉ BRETON I have the lowest opinion of erotic literature (for me, Sade or Louÿs are not erotic literature). To give a name to what one is talking about seems to me to be the least one can do. With some difficulty, but even with the woman I love (who doesn't like me to do so), I call a cock a cock, a cunt a cunt and so on.[2]

PAUL ELUARD Valentin, since you use words that are supposedly obscene during lovemaking, can you tell me how you justify them? Sexually?

ALBERT VALENTIN Sexually unjustifiable. I have loved two women in succession, the only two, one of whom wouldn't tolerate my using such words – I used substitutes – while the other demanded that I use them. I much preferred the second solution. Now that it's become a habit, I've continued with women I don't love.

ANDRÉ BRETON A problem for Eluard: you receive an anonymous letter in the post which contains a pair of woman's pants and a sheet of notepaper with the words 'I love you'.

ALBERT VALENTIN Are the pants new or have they been worn?

ANDRÉ BRETON That has no bearing on the question I addressed to Eluard.

PAUL ELUARD I'd throw them away.

ANDRÉ BRETON It's the word 'anonymous' which struck him. The pants belong to a woman you haven't seen for a long time.

PAUL ELUARD In that case, I'd keep them whatever happened. If it was from the woman I love, and if I wanted to see her again, it's inevitable that I'd see her. If it was from a woman I'd liked and who'd left me with a good memory, I'd be very touched.

ANDRÉ BRETON If I received an anonymous pair of pants, it would make me extremely uneasy. It would really spoil my life. Dreadfully serious.

PAUL ELUARD I'd throw them away.

Breton, are you always responsive to the love a woman has for you?

ANDRÉ BRETON Pessimism makes me believe that I'm never responsive to anything else and have never been responsive to anything else. I delude myself to the contrary, every time.

GEORGES SADOUL Certainly not in some circumstances . . . No . . .

PAUL ELUARD I mean that you'd go to bed with the woman who loved you . . .

ANDRÉ BRETON That was not how I understood the question. My answer would be no.

GEORGES SADOUL Similarly no, if it was a woman whom I didn't love.

ANDRÉ BRETON Valentin, what do you think of the idea of masturbating and coming in a woman's ear?

ALBERT VALENTIN I wouldn't dream of it.

ANDRÉ BRETON A purely surrealist question.

PAUL ELUARD I've already done it. It's very good . . . No, not very good, it depends.

GEORGES SADOUL I've never done it, but it appeals to me.

ANDRÉ BRETON It would only satisfy one side of the woman. The world is badly made.

PIERRE UNIK The ear is made for the tongue, not for the cock.

ANDRÉ BRETON See Molière . . .

GEORGES SADOUL And in the nose?

PAUL ELUARD I wouldn't like that. I hate noses. A complex. I'm against.

PIERRE UNIK See Courteline.[3]

PAUL ELUARD Does Breton enjoy licking a woman's eyeball?

ANDRÉ BRETON I would very much like to be a vampire, an incubus, etc. But life doesn't leave me enough time to lick eyeballs, etc.

PAUL ELUARD It's not a matter of having time, but it's something I've always done and which is remarkably enjoyable.

GEORGES SADOUL It's absolutely disgusting.

PAUL ELUARD It's absolutely admirable.

ANDRÉ BRETON Sadoul, what do you think of the idea of having breakfast every day with a very desirable, naked woman, sitting opposite you, whom you are absolutely forbidden to touch?

GEORGES SADOUL Yes. I would enjoy it, undeniably. I'd prefer it to breakfasting alone.

ALBERT VALENTIN I'd rather miss breakfast. Unbearable. I'd have an erection and I wouldn't be allowed to touch the woman! Out of the question. I never visit the Louvre, either.

PIERRE UNIK I'm currently pessimistic enough to say yes, I'd perhaps find it better than sleeping with a woman in most cases.

ANDRÉ BRETON That's absurd.

PAUL ELUARD I have always wanted that and many other similar things; it certainly wouldn't give me an erection any more than if she was dressed.

ANDRÉ BRETON I will write a book about it, one of these days.

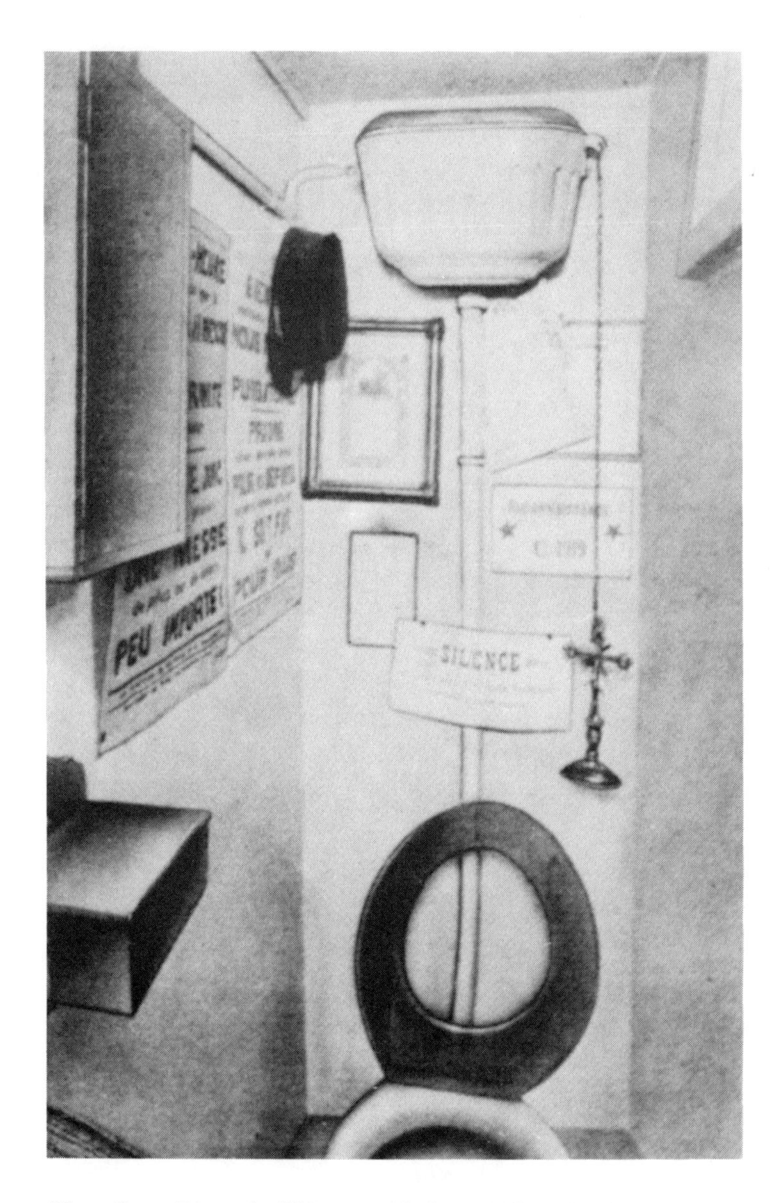

The toilet at 54 rue du Château, with the crucifix stolen from a church in Gers (see entry on Jean Caupenne in 'Notes on Participants'). Photograph by Man Ray.

Twelfth Session

1 AUGUST 1932

André Breton

Paul Eluard

Gui Rosey

Yves Tanguy

GUI ROSEY Is a woman's orgasm more intense than a man's? Breton?

ANDRÉ BRETON Less intense.

PAUL ELUARD Don't know.

YVES TANGUY Less violent, but longer.

GUI ROSEY Much more violent and longer. Favourite places to caress, for Eluard, in order of preference (first, with a woman you haven't had before)?

PAUL ELUARD None. Let the woman caress me. On the breast.

GUI ROSEY Jesus! Egoist. If Breton would permit me to ask him the same question.

ANDRÉ BRETON None. At the woman's initiation.

YVES TANGUY [. . .] [1] The anus + ...[2].

PAUL ELUARD How do you reconcile your love for the woman and your taste for sodomy? (A taste for sodomy being generally homosexual, the woman only being distinguished by her genital difference and not by her similarity in the rear.)

GUI ROSEY I like women with small buttocks between which the organ can be inserted as easily as into the vagina. In these cases, I double my pleasure by the tightness of the anus and at the same time it enables me to stroke the woman's clitoris.

YVES TANGUY Sodomy isn't homosexual. It's because it's a woman that it appeals to me. No explanation.

ANDRÉ BRETON [The question of] reconciliation doesn't arise. I prefer sodomy first and foremost for moral reasons, principally nonconformism. No child with a woman one doesn't love. With a woman I love, her self-abandon seems to me infinitely more moving in this form.

PAUL ELUARD Why?

ANDRÉ BRETON From a materialist angle, in the case of the woman I love, it is infinitely more pessimistic (law of shit) and consequently more poetic.

PAUL ELUARD Why, for example, does the idea of conception through coitus not seem to you more pessimistic than shit?

ANDRÉ BRETON Because it conforms to the idea of becoming which for me is indistinguishable from the idea of good.

PAUL ELUARD In the moment of coitus the two beings, for me, are an end in themselves and reproduction represents evil.

ANDRÉ BRETON A very Christian idea of the question.

GUI ROSEY Do you not believe that: (1) from the point of view of passion and precisely in order to give oneself entirely to the loved woman and for her to do the same, one must systematically eliminate the idea of reproduction? (2) From the strictly materialist point of view, procreation is to be absolutely avoided? (3) One should confine oneself to masturbation?

ANDRÉ BRETON (1) I thought that for a long time. I believe that it is that kind of error that has definitively ruined my life. (2) No. (3) Theoretically, under the present conditions of life and if love could overrule other determinants, yes.

GUI ROSEY Given your intellectual worth, would you not be grievously hurt by the bringing into the world of a child of yours whom you would find inferior, inadequate in comparison to yourself?

ANDRÉ BRETON It could not be the child of the woman I love. Which said, better that it should be inferior.

PAUL ELUARD Could you abide an *exclusive* regime of fellatio?

ANDRÉ BRETON No.

YVES TANGUY No.

GUI ROSEY No.

PAUL ELUARD What about an *exclusive* regime of sodomy?

ANDRÉ BRETON No.

YVES TANGUY No.

GUI ROSEY No.

Appendices[*]

*The Appendices have been assembled with the help of Josette and Jean Schuster

APPENDIX I

General Observations

This volume is based on twelve transcripts in manuscript form held in the André Breton archives. The first ten are dated, often by Breton – with the note '1st session', etc. – and paginated. The last two are dated but not paginated. We can surmise that after November 1930 there were further sessions which were not transcribed – or whose transcripts have been lost or destroyed, or still exist in other collections.

According to Marcel Duhamel in *Raconte pas ta vie* (Paris 1972), Max Morise acted as secretary, but he only participated in the first, third and fourth sessions. In various places it has been possible to identify the handwriting of Breton, Eluard, Péret and André Thirion. We would like particularly to thank Paule Thévenin, who enabled us to decipher certain pages that were practically illegible.

In all, forty people took part in these twelve sessions. But the number of participants varied considerably, ranging from four in the twelfth session to fifteen in the ninth. Only Breton was present on all twelve occasions. Unik attended ten times; Yves Tanguy, seven; Prévert, six; Duhamel, Eluard and Péret, five; Noll, Queneau and Sadoul, four; Morise and Valentin, three; and Aragon, Boiffard, Naville, Jeannette Tanguy, André Thirion and Vion, twice each. All others participated once only.

According to Pierre Naville in *Le temps du surréel* (vol. 1, Paris 1977), the first two sessions were held at 54, rue du Château, an important address in the history of surrealism, then lived in by Marcel Duhamel, Jacques Prévert and Yves Tanguy. It was Naville who first pointed out to Breton that the absence of women from the discussions would seriously detract from their value.

Women took part only in the three sessions of November 1930 – the eighth, ninth and tenth. In all, seven women contributed to the research: Nusch (who would marry Eluard in 1934), Jeannette Tanguy, Madame Unik, Simone Vion, Madame Léna, Katia Thirion and a mysterious 'Y'.

The first seven sessions were all held in the space of just over three months, from 27 January to 6 May 1928. The next three took place more than two years later, all in November 1930. The ninth is dated 26 January 1931, and the twelfth, 1 August 1932.

Transcripts of the first two sessions only, dated respectively 27 and 31 January 1928, were published in *La révolution surréaliste*, no. 11, 15 March 1926, and concluded with the phrase, 'To be continued' – a promise never kept until now.

Appendices II to VI detail further surrealist inquiries into sexuality.

APPENDIX II

Inquiry (1929)[1]

If there is one idea which to this day seems to have escaped every attempt at reduction and which, far from incurring their wrath, has defied the greatest pessimists, it is, we believe, the idea of *love*, alone in its capacity to reconcile every man, temporarily or not, with the idea of *life*.

This word, love, upon which buffoons have strained their coarse wits to inflict every possible generalisation and corruption (filial love, divine love, love of the fatherland), we are here, needless to say, restoring to its strict and threatening sense of total attachment to another human being, based on the imperative recognition of truth – *our* truth 'in a body and soul', the body and soul of this human being. What we mean here is that sudden renunciation, in the course of the quest for truth which is the foundation of all valid activity, of more or less patient systematic investigation, because of, and in favour of, a manifest fact which we had done nothing to produce and which, on a particular day and with a particular face, became mysteriously incarnate. These words will, we hope, dissuade from answering us all professional 'pleasure'-seekers, womanisers and playboy sensualists, no matter how inclined they may be to give a lyrical disguise to their manias, as well as the deriders and 'doctors' of so-called love-madness, along with all the inveterate imaginary lovers.

It is from the others, those truly conscious of *love's drama* (not in the childishly doleful but in the pathetic sense of the word) that we await a response to these brief questions:

I. What kind of hope do you place in love?

II. How do you envisage the passage from the idea of *love to the* fact of *loving?*

Willingly or not, would you sacrifice your freedom for love? Have you done so? If in your eyes it was necessary in order to keep faith with love, would you consent to sacrifice a cause which you had hitherto believed yourself bound to defend? Would you accept not becoming what you could have become if that was the price to be paid for fully abandoning yourself to the certainty of loving? How would you judge a man who went as far as betraying his convictions in order to please the woman he loved? Can such a forfeit be asked, obtained?

III. Would you accord yourself the right to deprive yourself for a certain time of the presence of the person you love, knowing how much absence can inflame love, yet realising the mediocrity of such a calculation?

IV. Do you believe in the victory of love's glory over the sordidness of life, or in the victory of the sordidness of life over love's glory?

Responses from: *Action française*, *L'Intransigeant* (Roger Vitrac), *Paris-Midi* (Noël Sabord), *Comœdia, L'Éclaireur de l'Est* (Andhrée Huguier), *L'Esprit français* (Francis de Miomandre), Jules Rivet, Jacques Baron, Clément Vautel, Luc Durtain, Fernand Marc, Blaise Cendrars, Mambour, Pierre Renaud, Jacques Delmont, M.G., Ferdinand Divoire, Hubert Dubois, Paul Ackermann, Laurens Van Kuyk, Robert Desnos, Roland Penrose, A. Blancaymes, Claude Estève, René Char, Roch Grey, Louis de Gonzague Frick, Valentine Penrose, E. Gengenbach or Jean Genbach, Victor Servranckx, François Ribadeau Dumas, *Raison d'être*, André Gaillard, Joë Bousquet, Maurice Heine, J.-H. Rosny senior, Maxime Alexandre, André Breton, Luis Buñuel, René Crevel, Paul Eluard, Max Ernst, Marcel Fourrier, Camille Goemans, René Magritte,[2] Paul Nougé, A. Rolland de Reneville, Marco Ristitch, Georges Sadoul, André Thirion, Pierre Unik, Albert Valentin.

APPENDIX III

Inquiry (1933)[1]

. . . Beautiful as the chance encounter on a dissection table of a sewing-machine and an umbrella!

LAUTRÉAMONT, *Les chants de Maldoror*[2]

Can you say what was the essential encounter of your life? How far did you think, and do you think, that this encounter was fortuitous? Necessary?

– ANDRÉ BRETON, PAUL ELUARD

If the response to this inquiry (140 replies to some three hundred questionnaires sent out) may be considered highly satisfactory in terms of quantity, we could not claim with any justice that all its objectives have been attained nor, in particular, that the concept of the encounter has emerged brilliantly elucidated. Nevertheless, the very nature of the views we received, the manifest inadequacy of the majority and the reticence or vacillation of a good proportion of those which did not purely and simply 'miss the point', confirm our feeling that on this topic there is room for an interesting survey of contemporary thought.

It is our belief that even the uneasiness provoked by a continuous and rather attentive reading of the pages which follow – which nonetheless contain some very valuable testimonies and which are shot through with brief shafts of light – bears witness to a deep anxiety rendered all the more significant by the fact that our average correspondent could not acknowledge it. In all probability, this anxiety expresses the present, paroxystic disorder of logical thought confronted by the fact that while order, finality, etc., in nature have no objective identity with their forms in the human mind, it can still happen that natural and human necessity come together in such an extraordinary and turbulent way that the two determinants prove to be indistinguishable. Chance having been defined as 'the encounter of an external causality and an internal finality', the question is whether a certain kind of 'encounter' – here, the essential encounter, that is, the supremely subjective one – can be conceived of under the heading of chance without immediately begging the question. This was the most enticing trap laid by our questionnaire. The least we can say is that few people avoided it.

But it was hardly malicious of us to count on obtaining from everyone we approached an extremely unreserved response by this sudden and undirected appeal to the memory dearest to their hearts. We knew that in this way we could indulge a desperate need for confessions and secrets whose satisfaction could only lead – with good or ill humour – to some sort of philosophical discussion. Our first question tended essentially to awaken certain minds to the field of affectivity, just as our second, by its nature, would lead them back to the field of absolute objectivity and detachment – which is why we put them so tersely. It could be said that our intention was to provide the mental equivalent of a hot and cold shower. We were far from disappointed by the results: in some cases, one question would indeed appear to exclude the other, sensitivity overriding rigour or alternatively ceding to it, with every abstention presenting its own distinctive quality. In every case, the problem we evoked, awakening it from its abstract existence in the depths of literature, took on a passionate life.

If we leave aside one of the pitfalls of any inquiry such as this one, the fact that those who take part are almost exclusively professional writers, along with a few artists, which removes any statistical significance, we must also recognise that once we are dealing with a subject like the one concerning us here, the methodological principle of our intervention carries certain dangers. In particular, our fear of paralysing many of our interlocutors by trying to establish an agreed, precise meaning for the words 'necessary' and 'fortuitous' (which would have entailed justifying and thus upholding our own conception) inevitably fostered a degree of ambiguity. Perhaps we still underestimated this ambiguity, for, as will be seen, some respondents believed they could derive the 'necessity' of the encounter from its hypothetically ascribed 'essential' character: an entirely pragmatic necessity which we had certainly not envisaged, and moreover one founded solely on a piquant truism.

We had aimed to place the debate on a significantly higher level, in fact at the very heart of that doubt which seizes the mind when one attempts to define 'chance'. We began by considering the concept's rather slow evolution up to now, starting in Antiquity with an 'accidental cause of exceptional or accessory effects taking on the appearance of finality' (Aristotle), going on to an 'event brought about by the combination or encounter of phenomena belonging to independent series in the order of causality' (Cournot),[3] via an 'event rigorously determined but such that an extremely small variation in its causes would have produced a considerable variation in its occurrence' (Poincaré),[4] and arriving finally at the definition of the modern materialists, according to whom (if we may boldly venture to interpret and reconcile Engels and Freud) *chance would be the manifest form of external necessity which traces its path through the human unconscious.*[5] Suffice it to say that our question was meaningless unless one recognised our intention of emphasising the ultra-objective side (corresponding simply to an admission of the external world's reality) which the definition of chance has tended to acquire historically.

For us it was a matter of discovering whether one encounter, chosen from the store of memory, whose circumstances, through the light of affectivity, subsequently acquired a particular prominence, had been, for those who chose to relate it, originally placed under the sign of the spontaneous, the indeterminate, the unexpected, the unpredictable or even the unlikely, and, if this were so, how these assumptions had been subsequently narrowed down. We relied on every observation, however absent-minded or apparently irrational, which could have been made on the conjunction of circumstances which prevailed in such an encounter to reveal that this conjunction is not at all inextricable, and to indicate the links of dependency which unite the two causal series (natural and human) – links which may be subtle, fleeting, disturbing to knowledge in its present state, but which can sometimes throw a dazzling beam of light on to man's most faltering steps.

Responses from: Ferdinand Alquié, Dr Alfred Appel, Arp, Jean

Audard, Audiberti, Marcel Aymé, Henri Baranger, Jean Bastia, Louis Bauguion, Jules Berry, Professor Marc-Levi Bianchini, Princess Bibesco, André Billy, Binet-Valmer, Jean-Richard Bloch, Gus Bofa, Sylvain Bonmariage, Saint-Georges de Bouhélier, Jacques Boulenger, Joë Bousquet, Kay Boyle, Brassaï, Claude Cahun, Roger Caillois, Georgette Camille, Pierre Caminade, Bernard Causton, Marc Chagall, Marcelle Chantal, Alice Cocea, Dr Codet, Armand Colombat, Benjamin Crémieux, André Cresson, Curnonsky, Damia, Daniel-Rops, Léon Deffoux, André Delons, Fernand Demoustier, Anne Denis-Dagien, Gaston Derycke, Lucien Descaves, Charles Despiau, Jacques Deval, Fernand Divoire, Dranem, Pierre Drieu La Rochelle, Marie Dubas, Hubert Dubois, Édouard Dujardin, Luc Durtain, Dussane, Mélot du Dy, Marcel Espiau, Gabrielle-Camille Flammarion, Fernand Fleuret, Florelle, Louis de Gonzague-Frick, J. Frois-Wittmann, Alberto Giacometti, E. Gimenez Caballero, Ed. Goerg, Roch Grey, Dr Lucien Graux, Maurice Heine, Franz Hellens, Maurice Henry, Georges Hugnet, Aldous Huxley, Max Jacob, Marcel Jean, Marcel Jouhandeau, Professor C.-G. Jung, Kandinsky, Count Hermann de Keyserling, René Lalou, André Lebey, Lotte Lehmann, Mme E.-L. B. Leroy, J. Lipchitz, Domingo Lopez Torres, Germaine Lubin, Guy Mangeot, Victor Margueritte, Jean-Daniel Maublanc, André Maurois, Maxa, Jehan Mayoux, Francis de Miomandre, J.-M. Monnerot, Marguerite Moreno, C. Moricand, Dr E. Osty, Marianne Oswald, Dr C. Parcheminey, A.-M. Petitjean, Louis Piérard, Léon Pierre-Quint, Georges Pitoëff, Ludmilla Pitoëff, Ezra Pound, Gaston Pulings, Man Ray, Paul Raynal, Dr Reber, A. Rolland de Renéville, Pierre Reverdy, S.A. Rhodes, Professor Charles Richet, Carlo Rim, Marco Ristitch, Jules Rivet, Francis Rolf-Schuler, Gui Rosey, Georges Rouault, Noël Sabord, Saint-Pol-Roux, Théo Schmied, W.B. Seabrook, Joseph de Smet, Fortunat Strowski, Emilio Terry, Germaine Thévenin, Ernst Toller, Henry Torrès, Gilbert Trolliet, Ninon Vallin, Clément Vautel, Andrée Viollis, Dr Paul Voivenel, Hans Waxman, Jean Wahl, Paul Westheim, Pierre Yoyotte, Émile Zavie.

APPENDIX IV

An Inquiry into Striptease (1958–59)[1]

In his book *Mythologies*, recently published by Seuil, Roland Barthes denounces what he calls the 'mystifying' aspect of striptease, which, under the guise of inducing and inflaming desire, tends to dispel it by the use of exoticism, dance, music-hall trappings (furs, feathers, tinselled g-strings), etc. Do you believe, like him, that, despite the protests it arouses from 'respectable' people (and which at best help to promote it), striptease in fact 'desexualises' the woman and restrains the necessary spontaneity and inventiveness of her amorous imagination?

Questions for Women

I. During a strip-show, along with observing the reactions of those around you, are you aware of learning a lesson which you could put to your own use? What is it? Is it something that could influence your own behaviour in love?

II. Have you felt drawn to identify yourself with the stripper, and to what extent? If not, have you derived any satisfaction from examining her body or her performance with a critical eye? With hostility?

III. Would you be interested in men methodically undressing on stage (even while of course wanting some quite different ceremonial, to be defined) – men chosen for their impressive bearing or for their real or imagined attractiveness?

Questions for Men

I. Do you consider striptease more or less effective than film in 'arousing the erotic appetite'? Why?

II. In terms of the effect they produce on the mind and senses, do you place erotic books – which aim to inflame the reader's imagination – above or below striptease, which claims to offer the excitement of a concrete erotic image which the other spectators can enjoy at the same time as you?

III. Does striptease reveal to you an area of temptation which with the complicity of the woman you love you could envisage enjoying – or would like to enjoy – in your own intimate life?

Responses from: Henri d'Amfreville, Hans Bellmer, Roger Caillois, Ado Kyrou, Françoise de Ligneris, Joyce Mansour, Nora Mitrani, Pierre Molinier, Edgar Morin, Michèle Perrein, Max Walter Svanberg, Monique Watteau, *Le surréalisme, même*, no. 4, Spring 1958.

Responses from: Robert Droguet, Nelly Kaplan, Meret Oppenheim, André Pieyre de Mandiargues, Zinaïde de Rachevski, Henri Raynal. Comments from Gérard Legrand: 'La Philosophie dans le saloon'. *Le surréalisme, même*, no. 5, Spring 1959.

APPENDIX V

An Inquiry into Erotic Representations (1964–65)[1]

The ingenuity expended in enumerating the positions of partners' bodies during the act of love contrasts sharply with the silence over the positions of their minds, and over the imaginary representations which they attach to the objective world. Would we believe in the words of love if they did not carry the hope of that union of the real and the imaginary of which the lovers' encounter forms the allegory? It is not without interest that imagination can substitute an absent (unobtainable, better loved?) partner for the real one. But such an eclipse is merely a single example. Let us remember that the power of the poetic image increases in direct proportion to the distance which normally separates the objects it brings together.

We would be grateful for your answers to the following questions:

How would you describe what you imagine during the act of love? Is it possible to apply value judgements to such images? Are they willed or spontaneous? Do they follow a fixed pattern? If so, what is it?

How do they intrude on the objective image you have of your partner? Of yourself? Of your surroundings?

Do the images which come to your mind during the act of love leave any trace in your everyday inner thoughts?

Do you believe they have a relationship to poetic creation?[2]

Responses from: Jacques Abeille, Jacques Brunius, Roger Cardinal,

Gérard Jarlot, Konrad Klapheck, Jean Malrieu, André Pieyre de Mandiargues, Pierre Molinier, Thérèse Plantier, Philippe Sollers, Max Walter Svanberg, Jean Zurfluh. Illustrations by Isabel Castellanos. In *La brèche, action surréaliste*, no. 7, December 1964.

Responses from: Guy Béatrice, Jean-Louis Bédouin, Raymond Borde, Adrien Dax, Robert Guyon, Christiane Rochefort, Her De Vries, Michel Zimbacca. Comments from Vincent Bounoure: 'Conclusion et feed-back'. Illustrations by Fred Forest, taken from *Barbarella*. In *La brèche, action surréaliste*, no. 8, November 1965.

APPENDIX VI

Introduction to the International Surrealist Exhibition (1959)[1]

To the Exhibitors

The International Surrealist Exhibition, to be at the Galerie Daniel Cordier from 15 December 1959 to the end of February 1960, will take as its theme *eroticism*.

In view of the present situation in the plastic arts, which must inevitably make one consider any distinction between the various declared tendencies (the most striking of which derive from surrealist automatism) to be rather vain, surrealism proper owes it to itself to reassert its rights in a domain, specifically its own, which runs no risk of being fragmented between increasingly modest and numerous exploiters and then shrouded in the vapours of technical problems. Although today 'nature' (in reference to the external world) is no longer, in art, invoked for its own sake, and is even dismissed entirely from the scene by some, there still remains a privileged place, a theatre of provocations and prohibitions, in which life's most profound urges confront one other. This place, into which surrealism has continually mounted expeditions from its earliest days onwards, is eroticism (which, of course, far from necessitating the depiction of scabrous scenes makes great use of ambiguity and lends itself to numerous transpositions). The fact is that it is here – and here alone – that between exhibitor and spectator, by way of a conveyed disquiet, the *organic liaison* which is increasingly lacking in the art of today has to be established.

This concept, which has always underlain surrealism, does not therefore imply any turning point in our outlook. At the very most we are taking it upon ourselves, faced with the present situation, to place a firm accent on those works, of the past as well as the present, which gravitate around carnal temptation and are thereby largely unamenable to the (increasingly defective) criteria of judgement applied to art today.

A game of individual exits and entrances, to which surrealism as an organised and durable movement is committed, makes it necessary to divide this exhibition into two parts: a *retrospective* part, comprising a selection of what are for our purposes and from our standpoint the most representative works of artists now outside surrealism: works chosen, however – as far as possible with the artist's agreement – from among those realized within the orbit of surrealism; and a *contemporary* part, for which we solicit an active collaboration in the project, one not limited simply to the sending of canvases, sculptures and 'objects' but extended here and now to the contribution of suggestions which may prove useful in determining the indispensable staging of the whole event.

The organisers also retain the possibility that they may call upon a small number of non-surrealist artists whose work, nevertheless, fits into the general framework of the exhibition.

To the Visitors

Following those of Copenhagen (1935), London (1936), Paris (1938), Mexico (1940), New York (1942), Paris (1947) and Prague (1948), the Eighth International Surrealist Exhibition, which takes place in Paris at the Galerie Daniel Cordier, from 15 December 1959 until 29 February 1960, is peculiar in that its theme is *eroticism*.

It goes without saying that the surrealist concept of eroticism rejects, to start with, anything in the nature of vulgar suggestiveness, an attitude which, as Georges Bataille has commented, 'represents an eroticism which is inhibited, transformed into furtive discharges, ridiculous pretences, allusions'. The unatonable sin of such an attitude is that it profanes mankind's greatest mystery.

It is Georges Bataille, again, who, in the course of an urgent and often moving investigation of the subject, has best succeeded in making us apprehend eroticism for what it is, that is to say an 'immediate aspect of inner experience, distinctly opposed to animal sexuality'. Bataille articulates these two great principles:

> 'Man's eroticism differs from animal sexuality in that it calls the inner life into question. *Eroticism is that part of man's consciousness which calls his own being into question.*
>
> *'The inner experience of eroticism demands every bit as great a sensitivity towards the anxiety which underlies the prohibition as towards the desire which urges us to violate it.'*

This prohibition, which has existed since time immemorial and continues to hold sway in every latitude over so-called 'savage' as over so-called 'civilised' races, is the true target at which eroticism aims its arrow. We have no doubt that it will become increasingly clear to the extent that we succeed in disentangling it from the dense undergrowth of prejudices which cover it. However, it would be idle to hope to advance here in the full light of day. Anyone who flatters himself on having braved prejudice *and* taboo simultaneously, without turning a hair, will find himself disqualified from dealing with eroticism, since his own consciousness has failed to realise eroticism's fundamental need for *transgression*.

In this respect, things are not really quite so black as Bataille has painted them, though this does not prevent his analysis from being absolutely valid for the extreme case. The triggering of eroticism in the human heart does not perhaps demand this overflow of contradictory energies in which only the pleasure-pain complement is capable of achieving sublimation through complete fusion. One is obliged here to emphasise the role played by individual constitutions and by the various formative influences – religious, moral – which, even when furiously rejected persist in undermining thought and life. R. Schwaller de Lubicz, brought up in disciplines very different from our own, and apparently unchafed by their yoke, is yet able to affirm:

> While the sense of shame and of aesthetics must be denied in eroticism, the sense of life and of the sacred cannot be denied without, at the same time, provoking the very negation of the erotic.

I have no doubt that from this point of departure an exhibition such as we propose will set out, with all the sense of adventure that the phrase evokes, to blaze a trail that will permit us to reconnoitre in the very heart of the virgin jungle of Paris itself, on the threshold of the year 1960. Whatever may be the hypocrisies with which it will certainly find itself confronted, nothing can alter the fact that the idea behind it is today very much 'in the air' (even though this expression has had currency for some time, only today has it become concretely and dramatically pregnant with meaning). Witness merely the thesis, evoking both the new ambitions nourished by mankind and the imminent threat of annihilation of the species, put forward in a recently published anonymous work entitled *Emmanuelle*:

> The only art which measures up to man in space, the only one capable of leading him beyond the stars, just as figures of ochre and smoke once opened the walls of his caverns on to the future, is eroticism.

Surrealism has never relaxed its vigilant survey of this vast ocean. Nothing can deflect it from its determination to face up to what is clearly recognisable on all sides as a 'sign of the times'.

First remark: Anyone undertaking to unravel the secret of the elective fascination which the entirely dissimilar works of Duchamp and de Chirico have been able to exercise with unabated power upon surrealism since its origin is likely to lose himself in sterile conjectures if he fails to realise that their highest common factor is *eroticism*. It should be noted that, in both cases, it is a question of a 'veiled' eroticism (the first perfectly deliberate, the second almost certainly involuntary) having recourse to two different emblematic structures. One might add that, over and above their extreme disparity of means and appearance, what in general characterises and qualifies any works of art as surrealist is, first and foremost, their erotic implications.

Second remark: Alcide Bonneau, prefacing Nicolas Blondeau's *Dictionnaire érotique latin-français* in 1885, writes:

> Despite all the reasons that may be put forward in favour of speaking frankly and avoiding prudery, I incline to share the aversion of many people towards those words which we are told are the language of love, but which smell bad and make dirty stains on the paper on which they are written.

It is indeed only at this price that eroticism, rescued from shame, can claim the high place to which it is entitled. Our deepest concern has been to banish such words – the representations they entail – from this exhibition.

– ANDRÉ BRETON

This Appendix was translated by Simon Watson-Taylor, revised by Donald Nicholson-Smith.

Notes on Participants

by Malcolm Imrie

Neither José Pierre nor I have been able to discover anything about Humm, Madame Léna, Victor Mayer (or Meyer), Schnitzler or Schwarz. Significantly enough, we know nothing either of Jeannette Tanguy or Madame Unik, save for their marital status. José Pierre suggests that Simone Vion was the companion of Albert Valentin. I have provided brief biographical details of other, lesser-known figures (drawing on José Pierre's own notes in the case of Baldensperger, Blum and Michelet). For those already well known, such as Breton and Eluard, I have given little more than their dates and selected bibliographies. Easily the most comprehensive reference work on surrealism is the *Dictionnaire général du surréalisme et de ses environs* (Adam Biro and René Passeron, eds, Paris, Office du Livre, 1982). The best introduction to surrealism in English remains Maurice Nadeau's *The History of Surrealism* (London, Cape, 1968 and Harmondsworth, Pelican, 1973 and 1978). Only a small fraction of the greatest surrealist writing has been translated into English, much of that thanks to Atlas and one or two other small presses.

MAXIME ALEXANDRE (1899–1976) Born in Alsace, Alexandre was an active member of the surrealist group from its foundation in 1924 until 1932 when he left, following the departure of Louis Aragon. He converted to Catholicism in 1949, though quickly distanced himself from the Catholic Church. As well as studies of the German Romantics, and histories of German and Alsatian literature, his published work includes: *Les desseins de la liberté* (1927), *Le corsage* (1931), *Cassandre de Bourgogne* (1939), *Durst und Quelle* (1952) and, both with illustrations by Jean Arp, *L'enfant de la terre* (1965) and *L'oiseau de papier* (1973). His *Mémoires d'un surréaliste* were published in 1968, and his *Journal 1951–1975* in 1976.

LOUIS ARAGON (1897–1982) Founder, in 1919, with André Breton and Philippe Soupault, of *Littérature*, a magazine which in its two series marked its editors' passage through Dada and the birth of surrealism. During the 1920s, Aragon was one of Breton's closest friends and shared his organisational role in the surrealist group, while publishing poetry and some of surrealism's most memorable prose (*Le paysan de Paris*, 1926; *Traité du style*, 1928). Together with Breton, Eluard, Péret and Unik, he joined the French Communist Party (PCF) in 1927. His relations with the group became strained following his participation – along with Georges Sadoul – in the Second International Congress of Revolutionary Writers held in Kharkov in 1930, where he signed a declaration condemning idealism, Freudianism and Trotskyism. Tensions were exacerbated by the start of his lifelong relationship with Elsa Triolet, who disliked surrealism and whom Breton regarded with suspicion. His final break from surrealism occurred two years later, after his prosecution for publishing the poem *Front rouge*, which, whatever its merits, owed more to the Comintern than to surrealism ('Kill the cops/comrades/kill the cops . . . Fire on Léon Blum . . . Fire on the trained bears of social democracy . . . Under the leadership of the Communist Party . . . You are waiting finger on the trigger . . . '). While Breton defended Aragon's right to publish it, he criticised it as retrogressive poetry. With Triolet, Aragon went on to become one of the PCF's most celebrated public figures, rarely criticising Soviet policy until the 1960s. With Eluard, he was one of the most popular Resistance poets during the Occupation (*Le crève-coeur*, 1941; *Les yeux d'Elsa*, 1942; *Le Musée Grévin*, 1943). He became the editor of the influential review *Les lettres françaises* in 1953, and published several novels, of which the most notable are *Aurélien* (1945), the six-volume *Les communistes* (1949–51), *La semaine sainte* (1958) and *Blanche, ou l'oubli* (1967).

ANTONIN ARTAUD (1896–1948) Born in Marseilles, Artaud came to Paris in 1920 and worked as an actor in the theatre and cinema (appearing in films by Pabst and Lang, in Dreyer's *La passion de Jeanne d'Arc* and Gance's *Napoléon*). He was a member of the surrealist group from 1924 until November 1926, contributing to *La révolution surréaliste* the inflammatory *Lettre aux recteurs des universités européennes*, *Lettre aux médecins-chefs des asiles de fous*, *L'adresse au Dalaï-lama*, etc. As his contribution to these discussions well illustrates, Artaud's ideas were incompatible with surrealism, but despite some bitter exchanges following his departure, he maintained his friendship with Breton. In 1926 he founded the short-lived Théâtre Alfred-Jarry with Roger Vitrac, and began developing the concept of a paroxystic, transformative 'Theatre of Cruelty', as elaborated in *Le théâtre et son double* (1938) and exemplified in his only full-length play, *Les Cenci*. His ideas on theatre drew on Balinese dance and Mexican Indian culture (his visit to Mexico and experiments with the drug peyotl inspired his text *Au pays des Tarahumaras*). In 1937, in a desperate material and emotional state, he was expelled from Ireland, arrested on his arrival at Le Havre, and moved from one hospital to another, finishing up in the asylum at Rodez in 1943. Released in 1947, he returned to Paris, published *Artaud le Momo*, *Van Gogh, le suicidé de la société*, *Ci-gît* and finally *Pour en finir avec le jugement de Dieu*, which he was to have broadcast on 4 February 1948. Despite public support from his friends, the broadcast was banned. Artaud died one month later.

JEAN BALDENSPERGER All that is known of him is that he came from the Vosges, and was one of the 'friends and sympathisers' who were asked to attend the famous meeting at the Bar du Château on 11 March 1929, held partly in order to discuss the treatment of Trotsky (who had just been exiled from the Soviet Union) but more broadly to clarify surrealism's ideological position. Baldensperger was one of six people who were excused for not replying to the invitation, since they could not have received it in time. During the meeting, Pierre Unik named twenty people whose revolutionary credentials he trusted, one of them being Baldensperger.

JACQUES BARON (1905–?) Sometimes called 'the Rimbaud of surrealism', Baron published his first poetry at sixteen, and collaborated with

Breton and Aragon on the first issue of *Littérature*. He joined the PCF in 1927 but soon moved towards Trotskyism. He was expelled from the surrealist group in 1929. He published his memoirs, *L'an I du surréalisme*, in 1969.

BAUER The only reference to Bauer I have found is in Thirion's *Révolutionnaires sans révolution* (translated as *Revolutionaries Without Revolution* by Joachim Neugroschel, New York, Macmillan, 1975). Describing the surrealist group in 1930, Thirion writes: 'With the autumn, a group of young vagabonds heaved into view. The most active was a man of vague nationality who said his name was Bauer, a sort of red-haired hippy. He may have been an illuminato, provocateur, or humbug; we were never to discover which.'

PIERRE BLUM Probably a member of the Comintern-controlled International Red Aid, Blum was a signatory of the petition protesting at Aragon's prosecution over the publication of *Front rouge*. Nothing is known of his subsequent career.

JACQUES-ANDRÉ BOIFFARD (1903–1961) An early member of the surrealist group, he published several automatic texts and accounts of dreams in *La révolution surréaliste*. His photographs of Paris were also published in the magazine and used as illustrations in Breton's *Nadja*. He left the group during the dispute which followed the Bar du Château meeting and, along with Morise, Baron, Queneau and Prévert, published a pamphlet in 1930, *Un cadavre*, bitterly attacking Breton. He went on to collaborate on Georges Bataille's journal, *Documents*, and later abandoned artistic activity for a career in medicine.

ANDRÉ BRETON (1896–1966) Surrealism's founder and principal theorist; the central figure in the movement until his death. Breton's first collection of poems, *Mont de piété*, was published in 1919; a year later he and Philippe Soupault produced the first example of the 'automatic writing' they had invented, *Les champs magnétiques*. His inaugural *Manifeste du surréalisme* appeared in 1924; from then on his life and the history of surrealism are inseparable. In 1927 he joined the PCF; he was expelled in 1933 for publishing an article in *Le surréalisme au service de la révolution* attacking the 'wind of cretinization blowing from the USSR'. He visited Trotsky in Mexico in 1938 and, together with Diego Rivera, they established the Federation of Independent Revolutionary Art. He spent most of World War Two in the United States, returning to France in 1946, where he continued to animate surrealist activity until his death. His major works include: *Clair de terre* (1923), *Les pas perdus* (1924), *Légitime défense* (1926), *Introduction au discours sur le peu de réalité* (1927), *Le surréalisme et la peinture* (1928), *Nadja* (1928), *Second manifeste du surréalisme* (1930), *L'immaculée conception* (with Paul Eluard, 1931), *L'union libre* (1931), *Le revolver à cheveux blancs* (1932), *Les vases communicants* (1932), *Point de jour* (1934), *L'amour fou* (1937), *Anthologie de l'humour noir* (1940), *Fata Morgana* (1942), *Arcane 17* (1945), *Ode à Charles Fourier* (1947), *La lampe dans l'horloge* (1948), *Flagrant délit* (1949), *La clé des champs* (1953), *L'art magique* (with Gérard Legrand, 1957).

JEAN CAUPENNE (1908–?) Little is known of Caupenne, who came from Lorraine, apart from a catalogue of invective against priests ('servants of the bearded whore of Nazareth') which he wrote for *La révolution surréaliste* No. 12, and an incident in which he and Georges Sadoul sent a postcard to a certain Keller, leader of his class at the Sainty-Cyr military academy, referring to him as 'a garbage can full of shit' and demanding his resignation. This led to Sadoul being sentenced to three months in prison (which he avoided by travelling to the Kharkov conference in the Soviet Union) and to Caupenne making a public apology. The whole episode was frowned on by the surrealist group, from which Caupenne then disappeared. In *Révolutionnaires sans révolution*, André Thirion recounts a raid on a church in the town of Gers which the two of them undertook in 1928. 'It was deserted, so we conscientiously pissed into the holy-water basins, filled the collection box with pebbles, and filched all the ornaments on the altar, including the crucifix. Opening the tabernacle, we removed the ciborium, which was filled with consecrated wafers . . . we mailed the whole batch to Monsieur Louis Aragon, poet, 54 rue du Château, Paris. . . . Our shipment met with success. When we came back, Aragon showed us how he used the stolen goods to decorate the toilets. . . . The crucifix functioned as a handle for the flush chain, and that little closet became one of the prime attractions in the place.'

MARCEL DUHAMEL (1900–77) Duhamel, who neither wrote nor painted, was surrealism's benevolent landlord: his house at 54 rue du Château in Paris was home during the 1920s to Prévert and Tanguy, and Péret and Queneau stayed there for long periods. He took part in all the group's activities until 1930, and describes the period well in his autobiography, *Raconte pas ta vie* (1972). But Duhamel is now best known as the founder of Gallimard's 'Série Noire' in 1945, which published American crime writers such as Hammett, Chandler, Thompson and Himes for the first time in France. Duhamel also translated, or co-translated, several books in the series, including Thompson's *Pop. 1275* and Himes's *If He Hollers, Let Him Go.*

NUSCH ÉLUARD (NÉE MARIA BENZ, 1906–46) Born in Mulhouse, she met Paul Eluard in 1930 while working as a model for sentimental postcards and as a walk-on at the Grand Guignol. She married him in 1934, and was associated with the surrealist group throughout the 1930s. She was a model for Man Ray, and was the creator of a series of photomontages between 1934 and 1936.

PAUL ELUARD (NÉ EUGÈNE GRINDEL, 1895-1952) One of the greatest French lyric poets of this century, Eluard was an influential figure in surrealism from its beginnings until 1938. At that time, particularly in response to the Spanish Civil War, he moved back into the orbit of the PCF (from which he'd been expelled along with Breton in 1933), rejoining it in 1942 and thereafter serving it faithfully. His collections of poetry include: *Mourir de ne pas mourir* (1924), *Capitale de la douleur* (1926), *L'amour la poésie* (1929), *La vie immédiate* (1932), *La rose publique* (1934) and *Facile* (illustrated with photos of Nusch by Man Ray, 1939). His Resistance poetry is collected in *Poésie et vérité* (1942), *Les sept poèmes d'amour en guerre* (1943) and *Au rendez-vous allemand* (1944).

MAX ERNST (1891–1976) Born in Brühl in Germany, Ernst studied philosophy in Bonn before taking up painting and becoming active in the Cologne Dada group. He moved to Paris in 1921, where he met Eluard and Breton, and was a member of the surrealist group from its foundation. Many of his major paintings were produced in the 1920s, including 'L'éléphant Célèbes', 'Œdipe roi', 'Famille nombreuse',

'Deux enfants sont menacés par un rossignol', etc. In 1925 he discovered the technique of *frottage*, by rubbing black lead over paper placed on wooden floorboards; he regarded the technique as the equivalent of automatic writing, and used it frequently in subsequent work, beginning with the collection *Histoire naturelle* (1927). Ernst also refined the use of collage, notably in a series of collage-novels which included *La femme 100 têtes* (1929), *Rêve d'une petite fille qui voulut entrer au Carmel* (1930) and *Une semaine de bonté* (1934). He lived with the English surrealist painter Leonora Carrington from 1937 until his internment at the outbreak of war. On his release he moved to New York where he edited the magazine *VVV* with Breton and Marcel Duchamp. He married the American artist Dorothea Tanning in 1946. He returned to Paris after the war, and was expelled from the surrealist group in 1954 for having taken part in the Venice Biennale, where he was awarded the Grand Prix.

RAYMOND MICHELET Michelet seems to have participated briefly in surrealist activities around 1930–31, as a friend of Sadoul and Thirion, who were by then living at 54 rue du Château. Thirion refers to him several times in his book, *Révolutionnaires sans révolution* (1972). According to Thirion, Sadoul introduced him to Nancy Cunard, who 'gobbled down that fresh body in no time'.

MAX MORISE (1900–73) Originally a Dadaist, Morise joined the surrealist group at the same time as his friends Baron, René Crevel, Robert Desnos and Roger Vitrac (with some of whom he had edited the magazine *Aventure* between 1921 and 1922). He chaired the meeting at the Bar du Château on 11 March 1929, and transcribed at least the first of the sessions in this book. He left the group at the end of the 1920s and was one of the signatories of *Un cadavre* (in which he wrote, 'If André Breton should take a fancy to pigs' feet *à la poulette*, you'll suddenly find these are confirmed revolutionaries.').

PIERRE NAVILLE (born 1903) Naville was born in Paris, where he still lives, and was an active member of the surrealist group from the start, co-editing (with Péret) the first three issues of *La révolution surréaliste*. He was the first in the group to raise seriously the issue of political commitment, most sharply in his 1926 pamphlet *La révolution et les intellectuels (Que peuvent faire les surréalistes?)* which presented his colleagues with a choice between pursuing 'a negative attitude of an anarchic order . . . a refusal to compromise its own existence and the sacred character of the individual . . . ', or taking a revolutionary, Marxist path. It was a choice which few of them were prepared to make (although the pamphlet helped to propel Breton, Aragon, Eluard, Péret and Unik into the PCF), and Naville moved away, becoming co-director of the Marxist journal *Clarté*, and finally leaving the surrealists in 1928, after a dispute with Breton over his decision to publish Victor Serge in the journal. Naville moved from support for the Left Opposition in the Soviet Union to becoming one of the founders of the Trotskyist Fourth International, but maintained his affinity for surrealism. He wrote an important study of socialist theory (*Le nouveau Léviathan*, vols I-VI, 1957–75) and many books on politics, sociology and psychology, as well as translating C.L.R. James's *The Black Jacobins*. In 1977 he published *Le temps du surréel*, which remains one of the most valuable accounts and assessments of surrealism.

MARCEL NOLL Little is known of Noll beyond the fact that he came from Strasbourg, and joined the surrealist group in 1924. He published accounts of dreams and automatic writing in *La révolution surréaliste*, and was briefly manager of the Galerie Surréaliste, before leaving the group in 1929.

BENJAMIN PÉRET (1899–1959) According to Robert Desnos, Péret's mother brought him to Paris and introduced him to Breton in 1920 ('Monsieur, I have heard all about you and I am told you could do something for my son who wants to embark in literature'): the two became lifelong friends. Péret published his first collection of poems, *Le passager du transatlantique*, in 1921. A founder of the surrealist group, he was surrealism's most intransigent revolutionary and one of its finest writers. He joined the PCF in 1926, and worked on its newspaper, *L'Humanité*, as a journalist and proof-reader (professions which he followed throughout his life, never scraping more than a precarious living), then travelled to Brazil in 1931 and became active in the Left Opposition. During the Spanish Civil War Péret fought alongside the Trotskyists of the POUM and later the anarchists of the Durruti division, till both were crushed in Barcelona by the Communist Party. Back in France, he was called up in 1940 (his first job was to compile a list of 'suspicious persons' which, true to his profound anti-clericalism, he did by removing names of political suspects and substituting those of local priests). Forced to flee Paris, via Marseilles, he moved to Mexico with his lover, the painter Remedios Varo (whom he married in 1943 on the death of his first wife, Elsie Houston), and there established a section of the Fourth International. He left the Fourth International over its attitude to the Soviet Union (adopting the view that it was a 'state capitalist' society). On his return to Paris in 1948, he renewed his surrealist activities, now particularly inspired by his deep interest in Central American myths and legends, while continuing his work as a militant in increasingly obscure Trotskyist factions, including the short-lived Union Ouvrière Internationale. His poetry includes: *Immortelle maladie* (1924), *Le grand jeu* (1928), *Je ne mange pas de ce pain-là* (1936), *Trois cerises et une sardine* (1937) and *Air mexicain* (1952). He also published several prose collections, including *152 proverbes mis au goût du jour* (with Eluard, 1925), *Au paradis des fantômes* (1938), and *Mort aux vaches et au champ d'honneur* (1953); and some anthologies and polemics, including *La parôle est à Péret* (1943), *Le déshonneur des poètes* (1945), *Anthologie de l'amour sublime* (1956) and *Anthologie des mythes, légendes et contes populaires d'Amérique* (1960).

JACQUES PRÉVERT (1900–77) Though Prévert was only a member of the surrealist group for three years (from 1925 to 1928 or 1926 to 1929, according to different accounts) and published nothing in *La révolution surréaliste*, his role in the group's early years, when he lived in the rue du Château household, was far from negligible. His departure was acrimonious, and he contributed to the pamphlet attacking Breton, *Un cadavre*. Subsequently, of course, Prévert became one of France's most popular poets, and many of his verses were set to music. He also wrote fiction and film scripts (he collaborated with Marcel Carné on *Quai des brumes*, *Le jour se lève* and *Les enfants du paradis*). His poetry was collected in the bestselling *Paroles* (1946).

RAYMOND QUENEAU (1903–76) Queneau's involvement in surrealism largely parallels Prévert's, although he was a more active member of the group, writing tracts and material for *La révolution surréaliste*. He left in 1929 (and gives a critical account of the group in his 1937 novel *Odile*).

Like Prévert, he is better known for his subsequent literary career than as a surrealist: for his poetry, parodies and inventive fiction, most notably *Zazie dans le Métro* (1959).

MAN RAY (1890–1976) Born in Philadelphia, Man Ray abandoned his studies in architecture and industrial design to take up painting, moving through abstraction to Dada. He came to Paris in 1921, exhibited his paintings and began experimenting with photography, using 'rayograms' and solarisation. He also worked in the cinema, acting in René Clair's *Entr'acte*, directing several films including *Emak Bakia* (1926), *L'étoile de mer* (1928) and *Les mystères du château de Dé* (1929), and later collaborating with Hans Richter on *Dreams That Money Can Buy* (1944). He was a member of the surrealist group, though not always an active one, from its foundation for most of his life.

GUI ROSEY (born 1896) A poet, Rosey joined the group in 1932 and was an active member until the outbreak of war. Having met up with Breton and Péret in Marseille he then disappeared, apparently first hiding in Provence and then becoming the roving European agent for a Czech manufacturer. He returned to France in 1960, and continued to publish poetry. His work includes: *La guerre de 34 ans* (1932), *Drapeau nègre* (1933), *André Breton* (1937), *Electro-magie* (1969) and *Les moyens d'existence* (1969).

GEORGES SADOUL (1904–69) A member of the group from 1926 to 1930 (leaving with Aragon with whom he had attended the Kharkov conference), Sadoul is now better known for his later work as a film historian and critic.

YVES TANGUY (1900–55) One of the greatest surrealist painters, Tanguy joined the group in 1925 and stayed in the movement for the rest of his life, contributing drawings and texts to most surrealist magazines, including *La révolution surréaliste, Le surréalisme au service de la révolution, VVV* and *Minotaure*, and providing covers and illustrations for many surrealist books (including Breton's *Anthologie de l'humour noir* and the surrealists' edition of Lautréamont's collected works). He emigrated to the United States in 1939, with his wife, the painter and poet Kay Sage, becoming a US citizen in 1948.

ANDRÉ THIRION (born 1907) A political theorist and writer, Thirion was an active member of the group between 1928 and 1934, at the same time as being a militant in the PCF, often acting as intermediary between the two. Much later he abandoned both surrealism and the Left, becoming a Gaullist, though his memoirs of surrealism, *Révolutionnaires sans révolution* (1972) are far from unsympathetic. He now lives in Paris.

KATIA THIRION Born in Bulgaria, she came to study medicine in Nancy, where she met André Thirion. She returned to Bulgaria – where she already had a husband – but in 1930 Thirion travelled there and persuaded her to return to Paris with him. They later married. She joined the PCF and worked with Elsa Triolet designing jewellery, later becoming a radio announcer.

PIERRE UNIK (1909–45) An early member of the group, Unik published his first surrealist text in *La révolution surréaliste*, no. 6 (March 1926). He was one of the five surrealists who joined the PCF in 1927 and with them assembled the pamphlet *Au grand jour*, defending this decision. In 1932, following the split with Aragon, he and Maxime Alexandre wrote the pamphlet *Autour d'un poème* – the poem being *Front rouge* – which led to their separation from the group. Unik subsequently divided his time between the cinema (he wrote screenplays for Luis Buñuel and Jean Renoir) and journalism (for *L'Humanité*). Captured in 1940, he escaped from a prisoner-of-war camp in Silesia at the beginning of 1945, but never made it back to France, disappearing in Slovakia.

Afterword

by Dawn Ades

The twelve sessions of the 'Recherches sur la sexualité' took place during two distinct periods: the first seven in the early months of 1928, which Maurice Nadeau described as surrealism's calm 'year of achievements';[1] the second and more sporadic series of five sessions between late 1930 and 1932, following the commotion of exclusions and departures announced in the *Second Surrealist Manifesto*.

Just two of the sessions were published at the time, in the penultimate issue (no. 11, 15 March 1928) of the first great surrealist journal *La révolution surréaliste*. Founded in 1924, the year of the first *Surrealist Manifesto*, *La révolution surréaliste* published its twelfth and final issue in 1929, so bringing to an end 'a kind of mental year that [had] lasted five years'.[2] *R.S.*'s irregular publication bore witness to 'a series of ideological crises and picturesque departures',[3] but each issue brought together the ideas, experiences and experiments that had for a moment united surrealism's participants. Automatic texts that responded to the first definition of surrealism as 'pure psychic automatism', arguments about its extension into the visual field, narration of dreams, experiments with language, or Artaud's inflammatory attacks on the pillars of bourgeois society – 'Open the prisons, disband the army', for instance, in the second issue (January 1925) – appeared side by side with theoretical discussions of the role of artists and intellectuals within the revolution. Gradually, the generalised notion of revolt that characterised the first years of the movement hardened into more direct political commitment, and Breton, Eluard, Péret, Unik and Aragon joined Naville as members of the French Communist Part (PCF). This marked not the cessation but the start of a new wave of struggles within the movement, as surrealism sought to maintain its autonomy and the right to continue its own particular investigations into ways of changing consciousness, the role of the unconscious within the social body, and the current state of language both visual and verbal.

Surrealism undertook a constant probing of contemporary philosophy, politics and psychoanalysis, as well as poetry. It also had its own strict, though in no sense conventional, moral imperatives, and anyone who transgressed was summarily dismissed: the *Second Manifesto*, published in the final issue of *La révolution surréaliste*, recorded the exclusion of a number of its members of the first period, such as Desnos and Artaud. But by then surrealism had established itself as the major intellectual and artistic force in France. In 1926 Aragon had published *Le paysan de Paris* and in 1928, the year of the first 'Recherches' on sex, Breton had published *Nadja* and *Le surréalisme et la peinture*, Aragon *Traité du style*, Eluard *Défense de savoir* – the list goes on. What is crucial to understand, though, is that surrealism cannot be reduced or summarised as a series of such master 'works'. Integral and inseparable from these were documents like the 'Recherches', which were just as much a part of the life of the movement.

In the trajectory that runs from the very first texts in *R.S.*, through such works as Breton's *Nadja*, *L'amour fou*, and *Arcane 17*, and thence to the International Exhibition of 1959-60, whose theme was eroticism, the erotic relation was a central surrealist concern. But this relation was, at the same time, more fraught and contradictory than some of the great surrealist formulations of *l'amour passionnelle*, whether visual or verbal, might indicate. The 'Recherches' reveal some of the complexity of surrealist attitudes to sex, and help to site them, specifically with regard to contemporary debates within the psychoanalytical and political fields.

These conversations were, and still are, astounding, unprecedented and unmatched in their frankness and intimacy. The exchanges burrow for answers to the conundrums of sex and desire through a close-up examination of the physical practices and psychological inclinations of this fluctuating group of friends, coming back always to the 'concrete facts . . . the most basic facts of love'. There were no women participants in the first series, apart from the mysterious 'Y' in the seventh session, who is clearly female; their absence was noted and regretted by, it seems, only Naville and Aragon. None of the prominent new male voices whose entry into surrealism was announced in *R.S.* 12 – Magritte, Dalí, Buñuel – took part either, although Dalí lost no opportunity in other fora to detail his sexual experiences or fantasies. Aragon, who finally defected from surrealism in 1932, took no part after the third session, and Eluard was only involved during the second period. André Breton, in fact, was the only person to be present throughout.

Transcriptions of the first two 'soirées', published at the back of *R.S.* 11, were, the review promised, 'to be continued', but when *R.S.* 12 appeared in December 1929, there were no more 'Recherches'. The surrealists' interest in love and in certain aspects of sexuality had, if anything, increased, even judging on the basis of this issue alone, and was blamed for the long non-appearance of the review: the first half page of *R.S.* 12 bore the red imprints of seven pairs of women's lips under the caption 'why *La révolution surréaliste* had ceased to appear.'

But it seems as if the 'Recherches' were regarded for a while as something of a failure – or at least that they may have fallen temporarily into abeyance because they failed to provide the evidence Breton had hoped to garner from an investigation of 'the concrete facts of love' in order to prove that both desire and *jouissance* in the union that marked this supreme experience of life were truly reciprocal. Instead of the 'Recherches', *R.S.* 12 presented an 'Enquête sur l'amour' (see Appendix II) which significantly occupied the former position of the 'Recherches' at the back of the review.[4] In place of the primary question, of the 'Recherches', which was, as Breton identified it, 'To what extent and how often can [a man and a woman making love] reach orgasm simultaneously?', there was now the question, 'What kind of hope do you place in love?' This is not just a romantic reformulation of the same question, and the change of attitude, or of expectations, is clearly signalled in the 'Enquête's' rejection of the 'patient investigation' of the 'Recherches'.

What we mean here is that sudden renunciation, in the course of the quest

> for truth which is the foundation of all valid activity, of more or less patient systematic investigation, because of, or in favour of, a manifest fact which we had done nothing to produce and which, on a particular day and with a particular face, became mysteriously incarnate.

Love, then, is not susceptible to any proof, other than the experience itself which is now construed as an act of faith. This abrupt closure in favour of something akin to mysticism raises the doubt that the 'Recherches' might have been instigated only to prove the poverty of that 'materialist attitude' which Breton had attacked in 1924 in the first *Surrealist Manifesto*. But this suspicion regarding the 'Recherches' is, I think, untenable for several reasons, and undervalues the complexity of surrealism at this juncture.

First, and most obviously, there is too much genuine urgency here, too much vitality and tension – as well as too many moments of merriment. The participants are far from taking a purely 'materialist' attitude themselves. Furthermore the 'Recherches' conform to a peculiarly surrealist genre which united the need for collective experiences with the pursuit of research that could be analagous to but was never identical with that of 'scientists'. Discussing the investigation of dreams and the unconscious, in the first *Manifesto*, Breton could thus write: 'If the depths of our mind contain within it strange forces capable of augmenting those on the surface, or of waging a victorious battle against them, there is every reason to seize them – first to seize them, then, if need be, to submit them to the control of our reason. The analysts themselves have everything to gain by it. But it is worth noting that no means has been designated a priori for carrying out this undertaking, that until further notice it can be construed to be the province of poets as well as scientists . . .'[5] One early instance was the phase of collective experiments in hypnotic trance, recorded in the 'Entrée des médiums', which was published in the proto-surrealist review *Littérature* in 1922. In a more or less intense form, meetings to debate particular issues were also a regular feature of surrealist life.

Such 'group research' was not a stable form, but its various manifestations had certain common characteristics and performed the function of forging a common identity, binding the community and reinforcing its exclusivity. In this respect it partook of the activity of the *jeu*, a constant throughout the life of surrealism, which, as Breton said in the introduction to the game *L'un dans l'autre*, served to 'strengthen the bonds that united us'.[6] Not all these experiments and games were a success: we know that the hypnotic trances had to be abandoned because they began to touch dangerous territory. But none, perhaps, were failures in the sense that the 'Recherches' were, in that they revealed such a measure of disagreement among the participants. This shook everyone, but above all Breton, because what was fast becoming the special province of surrealism – the 'privileged place' of sexuality – was here demonstrated to be the source of some deep conflicts. Take this exchange for example:

BRETON Must love necessarily be reciprocal?
NAVILLE I do not believe it is absolutely necessary . . . .
UNIK There is absolutely no need for love to be reciprocal.
PÉRET It does not have to be reciprocal.
BRETON It is necessarily reciprocal.

This evidently touches on the primary question quoted above, and serves to give an idea of the persistent contradictions at every level in the 'Recherches', from the statement of the 'basic facts' of individual practice and inclination to such generalisations about love as those in the above exchange. The other two questions that Breton singled out as of special significance, should the answer to the primary question be inconclusive, were those that opened the first session: 'A man and a woman make love. To what extent is the man aware of the woman's orgasm?'; and 'Do you have any objective ways of telling?'

First to be interrogated was the painter Yves Tanguy: Yes, he thought there were objective means of telling – but, the editor of the session noted laconically, 'We are not told what these are'. Subsequent responses similarly failed to elicit any 'objective way of telling'. As the sessions continue, the negative, uncertain or conflicting responses of the male surrealists to these questions sound a note of pessimism that rings against both the occasional loftier expressions of faith in either love or sensuality and against the more sensational and sometimes comic answers to such questions as how, how many, how often, with whom or with what, and so on. The absence of accord, and the failure to establish anything approaching objective validation by these methods seems, to judge from the 'Enquête', to have led to their temporary abandonment.

The 'Enquête' on love, then, was an attempt to restore equilibrium and confidence to this special field. But the 'Recherches', it should be recalled, were revived in 1930, and rather than seeing the 'Enquête' as an act of substitution or suppression it is probably closer to the truth to see the relationship between them as part of a surrealist dialectic. The 'profane illumination' that Walter Benjamin, surrealism's most perceptive critic in 1929, appreciated in works like Breton's *Nadja* or Aragon's 'incomparable' *Le paysan de Paris*, rested precisely on this dialectical relationship between materialist investigation and illumination. *Nadja* itself is the recording of a failure rather than of the cloudy glories of 'admirable love'.[7] Benjamin was acutely aware of the danger to surrealism of losing its materialist, anthropological side.

> Any serious exploration of occult, surrealistic, phantasmagoric gifts and phenomena presupposes a dialectical entwinement to which a romantic turn of mind is impervious. For histrionic or fanatical stress on the mysterious side of the mysterious takes us no further: we penetrate the mystery only to the degree that we recognise it in the everyday world, by virtue of a dialectical optic that perceives the everyday as impenetrable, the impenetrable as everyday. . . .[8]

His sharp words uttered in relation to the mystery of 'spiritualism' rather than of love nonetheless call attention to the need perceived by the surrealists to maintain some form of dialectical materialism in their investigations even in the face of Breton's 'mysterious' revelation in the passage which should now be quoted in full from the 'Enquête':

> This word, love, upon which buffoons have strained their coarse wits to inflict every possible generalisation and corruption (filial love, divine love, love of the fatherland), we are here, needless to say, restoring to its strict and threatening sense of total attachment to another human being, based on the imperative recognition of truth – *our* truth 'in a body and soul', the body and soul of this human being. What we mean here is that sudden renunciation, in the course of the quest for truth which is the foundation of all valid activity, of more or less patient systematic investigation, because of, and in favour of, a manifest fact which we had done nothing to produce and

> which, on a particular day and with a particular face, became mysteriously incarnate.

The purpose of the 'Enquête' was not just to reap confirmation of love's mysterious incarnations, but, having stated this as a fact, to examine its potential extension into the public realm of '*la vie sordide*' – a typically provocative reformulation of the conflict between love and duty (once so perfectly formulated in the alexandrines of French classical tragedy). There is a revealing assumption that any conflict is more likely to be experienced by a man than by a woman. Breton's own response is both an extraordinarily elegant solution and an indicator of the problem of identity: he prints Suzanne Muzard's responses as though they were his own.

The investigations into sex, starting in the year of the publication of *Nadja*, span a particularly turbulent period of surrealist activity. This was characterised by a simultaneous turning inward of the movement ('It is absolutely essential to keep the public from entering if one wishes to avoid confusion'[9]) and an insistence on the right to speak out on all issues. Breton's aim, moreover, was not just to maintain a balance between Freud and Marx, but to initiate activities which would allow opposition to the social regime to interpenetrate with the exploration of states of consciousness and unconsciousness.

> How can one accept the fact that the dialectical method can only be validly applied to the solution of social problems? The entire aim of surrealism is to supply it with practical possibilities in the most immediate realm of consciousness. I really fail to see – some narrow-minded revolutionaries notwithstanding – why we should refrain from supporting the Revolution, provided we view the problems of love, dream, madness, art and religion from the same angle they do.

This statement, manifestly provocative in the already congealing climate of the French Communist Party, and easily misinterpretable, would have been understood by the surrealists and their fellow travellers in the context of debates concerning the surrealists' attitude to political action and their insistence on the need to continue their own investigations autonomously and independently. Breton, Péret, Unik,

Eluard and Aragon had joined Pierre Naville as members of the Communist Party; but the *Second Manifesto* recounts Breton's difficulties with the tasks set for him by the Party, and argues that: 'The problem of social action . . . is only one of the forms of a more general problem which surrealism set out to deal with, and that is the problem of human expression in all its forms.' This evidently is not just a question of literary expression – in fact it is quite the reverse. Again, it was Benjamin who pointed out that the surrealists' writings were not literature but something else ('demonstrations, watchwords, forgeries, bluffs, if you will, but at any rate not literature'), that they were 'concerned literally with experiences, not with theories and still less with phantasms'.[10] At issue was the possibility of expression that would take account of the whole of the human psyche, not just as conscious, controlled thoughts and acts, but as encompassing hidden, subconscious areas which the surrealists took as manifested in dreams, and madness, and potentially accessible in some form. It was not a matter, of course, of the 'whole of the psyche' expressed 'as a whole', but of its entry however fragmentary or partial into recognition. For the surrealists 'hysteria' was a form of expression no less than automatic writing. The question of sexuality was of particular importance, and of course here they are in accord with and indebted to Freud. However, their approach and their conclusions were very different from his. As they saw it, rather than using analysis to restore man to a normality conditioned by and posited upon social order, they intended to explore the explosive possibilities of human expression, including sexuality. As Breton wrote in the *Second Manifesto*:

> Everything remains to be done, every means must be worth trying, in order to lay waste the ideas of family, country, religion. No matter how well known the surrealist position may be with respect to this matter, still it must be stressed that on this point there is no room for compromise. Those who make it their duty to maintain this position persist in advancing their negation, in belittling every other criterion of value. They intend to savour fully the profound sorrow, so well acted, with which the bourgeois public – inevitably prepared in their base way to forgive them a few 'youthful' errors – greets the steadfast and unyielding need they display to laugh like savages in the presence of the French flag, to vomit their disgust in the face of every

> priest, and to level at the breed of 'basic duties' the long-range weapon of sexual cynicism . . . .[11]

Breton has in mind here the stance of the social regime to sexual control: procreation within the family was seen as a patriotic duty in a country obsessed with a falling birth rate and fully reinforced by the still powerful Catholic Church. The 'sexual cynicism' Breton advocates should not be confused with 'libertinism' of any kind. Breton's form of 'surrealist sexual morality' did not tolerate the social double standards that assumed a function for prostitution; 'paid sex', as he described it, was anathema, and he speaks of dreaming of closing brothels.

But the surrealists' attitude to sex and the family was no less a cause of dissension with the Communist Party. The telegram to Moscow which re-affirmed the surrealists' commitment to the Third International and which was reproduced on the opening page of the new review *Le surréalisme au service de la révolution* did not announce any serious alteration of their methods of disruption and investigation. As far as the PCF was concerned the surrealists' courting of the erotic was indistinguishable from pornography. The eroticism of Dali's text 'Rêverie',[12] for instance, seemed gratuitous and perverse to them, and Breton was called on to denounce it, which he refused to do.

To detach love from the normalisation of sexuality within marriage, and to resist the construction of woman as mother, usually based upon the essentialist identification of woman with nature, were fundamental surrealist precepts. The surrealists' refusal of the family also implies a peculiar take on central tenets of Freudian theory. The long-range sexual cynicism directed at the bourgeois family and patriarchal power, evidently part of a social critique, also implies the rejection of the Oedipus theory that lies at the heart of Freudian psychoanalysis. As Foucault argues in *The History of Sexuality*, psychoanalysis rediscovered the law of alliance, with incest as the key to a sexuality that was constituted through marriage. Thus in the fourth session the exchange between Breton and Unik should be understood not as an assertion of the 'death of the father' but as denying that the child–parent relationship alone gives access to desire.

UNIK I do not believe anyone has the right to use the phrase 'to have children'. There are no fathers.
BRETON Children have no fathers . . . .[13]

The surrealists' embrace of the world of sexuality as a whole, however, shares with Freud the investigation of everything that had been labelled perversions; this included 'inversion', although the question of preference for members of the same sex led to the most dramatic conflicts within the group. The 'Recherches' probed what Freud called 'deviations in respect of the sexual object and the sexual aim',[14] such as fetishism, exhibitionism, scopophilia or masturbation. But they were not concerned with analysis in a Freudian sense, and were not therefore particularly interested in infantile sexuality. Sharing first memories of sexual awareness seems to have had little to do with a psychoanalytical rooting for suppressed or sublimated sexual forces, or to have been determined by Freud's notions of the origins of the sexual instinct and its phases of development.

Questions and answers on so-called deviations were posed and answered by the surrealists on the assumption that they had the value of a fact, rather in the same way that a dream had for them the value primarily of a poetic fact rather than a tool for analysis. And while Freud's interest in the relation between 'deviations' and 'what is assumed to be normal', as he put it, placed immense pressure on the concept of sexual normality, what he was in a sense doing was broadening rather than challenging the latter. Much of his evidence was based upon the observation of neurotic patients, and it was not until later that the research of sex investigators like Kinsey or Masters and Johnson into 'normal' sexual behaviour drew public attention to the problems of social assumptions about sexual control and morality and the realities of sexual behaviour and identity. Addressing the issue of female sexuality, more recent research has demonstrated 'both that female libido is hardly less – and may even be more – strong than male and that women are far more orgasmic than had been dreamt in Freudian psychology.'[15] Sexist in its methods as it may appear now, the surrealists' open challenge to the social control of sexuality necessarily opened a debate on female sexuality (see for instance the debate about 'clitorals' versus 'vaginal–uterines' in the seventh session). The surrealists' radical examination of sex runs parallel to the developments of psychoanalysis in France during the 1920s, and in a complementary manner both conditioned and was responsive to the shifting ground beneath notions of normality.

The first 'Recherches' published were subtitled 'The Place of Objectivity, Individual Determinants, Degree of Consciousness'. The promise or hope, therefore, was to examine sexuality simultaneously with regard to the possibility of objective knowledge and individual determinations. No other framework is proposed: indeed these investigations are pointedly placed outside a social or moral frame, though the question of a 'surrealist morality' does, as we saw, arise. They were clearly understood as an activity which by its very nature – private as it was – would help to ruin ideas of 'family, religion, country'. They also try to distance themselves from any framework that might be offered by the erotic or voluptuary. 'I have the lowest opinion', says Breton, 'of erotic literature (for me, Sade or Louÿs are not erotic literature).' The introduction to the 'Enquête' of 1929 offers another reason for the failure to publish the additional five sessions from the first period. The organisers wished particularly to discourage the attentions of 'professional "pleasure"-seekers, womanisers and playboy sensualists', as well as ' "doctors" of so-called love-madness' and 'inveterate imaginary lovers'. The first two sessions had, it would seem, aroused unwelcome interest from these quarters. The refusal to continue with their publication was less likely to have been due to a general fear of scandal – notwithstanding perhaps some individual demurrals regarding intensely private revelations and the probability of prosecution – than unease about the misleading light such a scandal would cast on the surrealists' objectives. 'The approval of the public', Breton wrote, 'is to be avoided like the plague.' As Benjamin, said, the bourgeoisie is as thick-skinned to scandal 'as it is sensitive to all action'.

The questions are posed in a quite anarchic fashion; sometimes they are answered systematically by all those present, sometimes one participant is put on the stand. Their very form precludes any systematic development of an argument. More than once if the conversation takes a turn Breton dislikes or disapproves he abruptly changes the subject.

Aragon, who has expressed moral and scientific outrage at the absence of women in the first sessions, is quick to pounce on Breton for his use of the term 'pathological'. The topic is that of the possible simulation of orgasm by the man. Several participants had sought to separate orgasm from ejaculation, and Breton has commented, 'Those can only be pathological cases'. Aragon responds: 'That seems to suggest that some of us believe in the idea of the normal man. I object to this idea.' The 'editor' or scribe at this point reduces the subsequent argument to 'approval from various participants', with Breton, Baron, Duhamel and Péret the only ones out of a group of thirteen men present to protest. The disagreement is over whether or not the idea of a 'normal man' has indeed been implied, rather than whether such a thing exists, a presumption that would seem to be against the spirit of the 'Recherches'. That they are perfectly aware of this debate is demonstrated in the final issue of *La révolution surréaliste*, in which J. Frois-Wittmann's 'Mobiles inconscients du suicide' was published. In a footnote, Frois-Wittmann there defined *l'homme normal* as 'a man who behaves as though he had been psychoanalysed', the only definition he found acceptable at the time. To this, one might contrast Aragon's comment on what he sees as the great contemporary problem in 'Introduction à 1930':

> The individual, who has long had some notion of his specific determinations, is suddenly confronted by an overarching social determinism that subsumes them. That is why I shall argue that what has characterised these last few years on the plane of modernity is the agony and the death of the essential individualism of the man of twenty years ago.

The three questions identified by Breton as primary are posited on gender difference, yet at the same time contain the desire to collapse this difference. In spite of the absence of female participants, the questions are in theory scrupulously posed to both. The first, in any case, was addressed indifferently to men and women; the second two were addressed to men, but then repeated with respect to women: 'To what extent' Breton asks, 'is the woman aware of the man's orgasm?' To which Morise replies with admirable honesty, 'I have absolutely no idea'. Pierre Naville had already protested against the absence of women, but this is the point at which Aragon actively intervenes. Duhamel has asked him the deplorable question: 'Does Aragon attach more importance to the man's orgasm than the woman's?' This question made explicit an assumption which Aragon complained of: that in some of the answers men and women were not treated as equal in sexual practice. As far as he was concerned, 'nothing can be said about physical love if one doesn't start from the fact that men and women have equal rights in it'. When Breton somewhat limply protests, 'Who has claimed the contrary?', Aragon explains: 'the validity of all that has been said so far seems to me to have been partially undermined by the inevitable predominance of the male point of view.' Inasmuch as the notion of reciprocity was the very basis of these investigations, and inasmuch as the questions sought to step out from narrow subjectivities, whether male or female, Aragon's protest was obviously justified. It is one of many signs that far from determining any measure of agreement, the investigations on the contrary were splintering any unity, and signs of tension within the group cluster round moments when the notion of 'normalcy' arises.

Although the three 'primary' questions are posited on the basis of a distinction between male and female sexuality, it was less a matter of examining this difference as such, to establish some kind of essential qualities to masculine and feminine sexuality, than of seeing how individual determinations could allow for mutuality in the experience of desire and *jouissance*. But the variety of other forms of attraction, sensuality, love and desire, including fetishism, bestiality, voyeurism, and homosexuality, often move the discussion into much more open and unstable areas. Discussion of the body viewed or touched, in those sessions where women are present, reveals differences of attraction and desire that do not group according to gender at all.

Breton's violent reaction against the discussion of male homosexuality in the second session is often instanced to the exclusion of Aragon's quite different response. As far as the latter is concerned, it is a 'habitude sexuelle' like any other, and attaches to itself no moral condemnation. Asked whether he condemns so-called perversions, Breton says not at all – with that one exception. The issue is discussed again at much greater length, with women present, in the ninth session. There is no consensus either among the men or the women, though much greater tolerance was expressed by the men towards female homosexuality. Bisexuality is quite widely accepted both in theory and practice, especially among the female participants. The resistance of some to male homosexuality is combined with pleasure at the representation of sex between females, which evidently interferes less with the imaginative construction of a masculine sexual identity.

The presence of women in the second series of sessions does not, if such was the intention, restore order and stability to notions of 'normal' male and female sexuality. When women are finally involved, in the eighth session, after a stilted beginning in which questions seem to have been posed in writing for the first time and manifest some obvious displacements of interest, those first key questions eventually arise again. As with the male surrealists, there is no measure of accord among them as to individual practice.[17] They frequently disagree with the men, but, while not silent, are in a sense mute. There was no question as to their full participation, equal sexual rights, or their right to speak openly of their own sexuality, which they do, but it is as though they are not heard, or, if they are, only to be contradicted: Breton, trying yet again to cast his net to trap and define the difference between male and female states of *jouissance*, provokes the following exchange:

VION There is the state of heightening pleasure, and there is the state of orgasm.
BRETON Even though we know that orgasm is a limit for us, how can we be sure that it is the same for the woman?
VION Personally, I think that when orgasm is over, I want to stop.
ELUARD Not all women think . . . .

The ambivalence of the surrealists' attitude to women, in terms of their treatment in the works of the male surrealists, their participation within the daily life of the movement and their struggle to find a space to be actively creative themselves, has come under considerable critical scrutiny. The male surrealists found it hard to accept that *l'amour fou* could be double-edged, and to perceive the contradiction that sexual liberty for the surrealist women still meant being trapped as the silent and often fetishised object of the gaze. Xavière Gauthier was one of the first, in *Surréalisme et séxualité*, to point to the phallicised language of sexuality in surrealism. She argues that if surrealism manifested a male heterosexual outlook in general terms, the work of many of its artists and some of its poets by contrast courted the perverse, which, in trying to subvert the 'law of the father', is 'a good place for the reversals and revolutions which allow cultural choices to progress'.[18] Gauthier feels that 'in surrealist poetry woman is good, and loved, but in surrealist art woman is bad and hated'.[19] 'Whether they idealized the female body and their love of it, as they did in their poetry, or attacked and dismembered it, as they did in their paintings, the male surrealists, according to Gauthier's analysis, were essentially using the woman to work out their rebellion against the Father.'[20] The radical nature of Gauthier's argument, which drew on Lacan and Bataille, detailing on the one hand surrealism's misogyny and on the other the perversity and transgressive nature of its sexuality as revealed in the works, was read at the time in France as an all-out attack on surrealism. But some who defended surrealism, like the book's *préfacier* J.-B. Pontalis, although finding parts of the argument incompatible, recognised that some of its discoveries could be to the credit rather than the discredit of the movement. The publication of the 'Recherches' opens up a far more complex picture of the sexual attitudes of the surrealists, both male and female, as of their conscious or unconscious assumptions about their own sexuality. This may be expected to provoke fresh consideration of the figuring of desire and the language of eroticism in surrealist works. Rosalind Krauss's argument, in 'Corpus Delicti', that the violence against and the fragmentation of the female body in surrealist photography starts a process of dismantling constructions of 'woman' is to an extent borne out by them.[21] To claim bluntly that the surrealists were misogynists seems to me to foreclose too abruptly on the surrealist investigations into sexuality.[22]

Magritte's *Je ne vois pas la (femme) cachée dans la forêt* was reproduced as part of the 'Enquête' of 1929 in *La révolution surréaliste* opposite his own response to the four questions the inquiry posed. These he answers in wholehearted orthodox surrealist fashion, with particular emphasis on one aspect of the questionnaire which was pertinent to his own practice as an artist. The hope he puts in love is precisely that of the second question – passing from the idea to the fact of loving: 'All I know about the hope I put in love is that only a woman is needed to make it real.' In the same issue of *La révolution surréaliste*, Magritte's fellow-Belgian Camille Goëmans writes in 'De l'amour à son objet' of the problematic of the stereotyping of the imagery of love: 'the pair of lovers turned in on themselves' could easily become a cliché, whereas 'the other image, which gives us love blindfolded, perhaps seeks to make us reveal more than we would wish'. Of course Magritte's painting-montage presents the 'woman' as the as-yet ideational object of male desire. But it is an oddly uncomfortable image of male desire, a curious, hands-off, detached vision in which the conjunction of naked and clothed does not function as an eroticising spark. The woman's half-gesture of *pudeur* is more of a self-absorbed caress than an act of self-protection. And the men, in the snaps taken in an automatic photo-booth, so flat, banal, and unlike the glamorous subjects of Man Ray's photo-portraits, are as isolated from each other as from the woman. And what of the oddly tacky nattiness of the men's clothes – they look tight, overdressed, uncomfortable in this bourgeois garb so unlike their usual one, with its ties, tight collars, jackets and overcoats. Trapped in this uniform, a little ludicrous, they seem to be Magritte's sardonic equivalent to the dramatic – almost hysterical – young man in Dali and Buñuel's *Un chien andalou* (the screenplay of which was printed in the same issue of *La révolution surréaliste*), battling with 'social' obstacles (priests, grand pianos) which prevent him from reaching the woman he desires. But the image also addresses a question which is frequently raised in the sessions in various contexts – for instance, that of masturbation: 'What representations accompany desire?'; the view was that this could not be an entirely imaginary figure. However, at other moments desire is figured as an ideal woman; in Aragon's *Le paysan de Paris* three surrealists walking together at night through the woods in the Buttes-Chaumont experience the same mirage of a woman 'so truly ready for anything that it would for her sake be worth the trouble of overturning the universe'. Magritte's painted woman, hidden, unreachable, the simultaneous object of the fantasies of all the dreaming males, might be the visual manifestation of that moment. Shared, this bond of desire does suggest an ambivalence, a sexual charge between the friends whose avowed object is removed to another realm.

The ambiguity of this image reflects interestingly on Breton's introduction to the International Surrealist Exhibition of 1959-60: eroticism, he writes, as 'a privileged place, a theatre of provocations and prohibitions, in which life's most profound urges confront one another', constitutes the only field, the only organic liaison that can bring together exhibitor and spectator. This conception, he goes on, 'has always underlain surrealism'. Breton is looking back over a quarter of a century of surrealist activity, and the ripe formulations, in this preface, of love as 'mankind's greatest mystery' and the untroubled acceptance of the erotic as the common denominator in works which are, as he says, at utterly different as those by Duchamp and de Chirico, tend to smooth over some of those earlier moments in the movement's history when issues of male and female sexuality and identity were urgently debated, meanings contested and individual practices upheld or condemned.

The relationship between sexuality and love was a cause of fierce disagreement in the 'Recherches'. At the extremes were Jean Genbach, defrocked priest with supposed Satanic tendencies, and Paul Eluard. The former, at the start of the fourth session, expresses his bewilderment that the surrealists could separate them: 'I am astounded by the fact that you are concerned with the sexual question on a physical level, that you can separate it from love.' Breton's perfunctory response, 'There has never been any question of making such a separation', glosses over the contradictions that this issue raised for him. Eluard, by contrast, in the eighth session, disagrees fundamentally with the direction in which Breton moves the discussion. He protests that 'This is an investigation of sexuality, not love'. He adds a little later that 'On all these questions I refuse to answer if we are discussing love'. He then qualifies this by asserting that 'Sensuality is something pure in which particular human beings cannot be taken into account'. For Breton, by contrast, sensuality is impure, and the argument continues through the next two sessions.

Although the surrealists were characterised by Bataille and the *Documents* group as poetic dreamers and evasive idealists who, it was implied in texts like 'The Language of Flowers',[23] were incapable of facing or responding to human baseness, this was more like a caricature of the complexity of their attitude. Breton charged Bataille in the *Second Manifesto* with a return to the old 'vulgar materialism'; Bataille called the surrealists 'base idealists' – deliberately bringing together 'base' and 'ideal', low and high, in an incompatible and repellent conjunction. But rather than affirming any constant elevation of a surrealist concept of love, there is in the 'Recherches' a constant interplay between pessimism and optimism, hope and despair, in the face of sexual experience. There is a revealing response from Breton, in the sixth session, following an outburst from Artaud against the satisfactions love was capable of bringing, and full of horror at the 'submission and depersonalisation' invoked therein. Breton, after repudiating the term 'satisfaction', goes on to say:

> If I place love above everything, it is because it is for me the most desperate, the most despairing state of affairs imaginable. My own depersonalisation in this realm is precisely all that I wish for. As to my submission, it is so bound up with domination that I am entirely taken over by it.

The scrupulous interrogation of 'concrete facts', as embodied in individual practice and inclination, could not entirely free itself of the contemporary discourse of sexuality in other fields, and indeed sometimes deliberately refers to it. One major instance of this is the response of the surrealists to the newly founded *Revue française de psychanalyse*, self-proclaimedly published 'under the high patronage of Professor Freud'. Freud's work was regularly published there in translation. Elisabeth Roudinesco suggests that the surrealists parodied the vocabulary of the 'listeners to sex', 'which gave their exchanges a technical cast . . . the poets translated their phantasms into a playful vocabulary – situating themselves in a kind of ongoing therapy allowing them to evolve an impassioned lexicon of love'.[24] Perhaps, too, they were being obliquely critical of that act of suppression whereby the analysts ignored their own sexuality while focusing on that of their patients.

There are also inevitably literary and poetic sources to some of the topics and individual responses in the 'Recherches'; Queneau is forced to admit, for instance, having described how he imagined two women making love, that he had no direct experience of such an event, and that his comments were 'livresque et imaginatif'. Although Breton explicitly distances their true subject of discussion from erotic literature, some responses are nonetheless evidently indebted to precisely that literature. Unik's notion of the abnormally large clitoris, for instance, can be traced to Sade's 'Sexual terrorists', as Angela Carter called them: phallic women like Madame Champuille in *The Hundred and Twenty Days of Sodom* or *Juliette*'s Durand. Sade, of course, as Breton said, was an exception. It was Sade's insistence on the free operation of desire, and on the transgressive value of perversion 'at the heart of a society that refuses and condemns it,'[25] that makes him in some ways the most important figure in the shadows behind 'Recherches.'

But one of the topics that most interferes with the credibility of witness for the contemporary reader is the surrealists' apparent fascination with succabacy. ('Succubus: a demon which according to popular belief takes the form of a woman in order to have commerce with a man'.[26]) The interest of the succubus for the surrealists – for which they inevitably drew on romantic diabolism from Baudelaire's '*succube verdâtre*' to Barbey d'Aurevilly's 'Le rideau cramoisi', one of the very few direct literary references in the entire 'Recherches' – lay partly in the challenge it posed to the imagination, or rather to the notion of a clear split between the real and the imagined. In the celebrated formulation of the *Second Manifesto*, 'Everything tends to make us believe that there exists a certain point of the mind at which life and death, the real and the imagined, past and future, the communicable and the incommunicable, high and low, cease to be perceived as contradictions'. The succubus figures in this twilight zone, and might also be seen in Freudian terms as exhibiting symptoms of the uncanny.

The question of the succubus arises in the course of a discussion of whether or not the representation of (a man or) a woman accompanies masturbation. Naville asks Péret whether he has experienced a sexual encounter with a succubus. Yes, Péret replies, and it's much better than masturbation. The difference he offers is that between a dream and the imagination in a waking state, but Breton criticises this as far too vague, and says that the difference is that there is no choice. For Breton, 'it is not a matter of a real woman'. Genbach, the defrocked priest, is clearly set up in the fourth session and tied in knots over the question of succubacy which, in spite of his pretensions, he fails to understand in surrealist terms.

Though this interest in succubacy may seem as deficient as their flirtation with spiritualism did to Benjamin, it is in fact a kind of private shorthand for the surrealists' quarrels with the contemporary practitioners of psychology and psychiatry, their radical questioning of socially governed definitions of insanity and their attack on notions of normal and pathological in sexuality. Breton's admiration for the Huysmans of *En Rade* and *Là-Bas* – with whom, he wrote in *Nadja*, 'I find so much in common about our ways of valuing the world, of choosing with all the partiality of despair among what exists,' – clarifies the role of succubacy in this context, for it provides the link with the phenomenon of hysteria. Breton and Aragon choose to view hysteria as much through Huysmans's eyes as through Freud's. Durtal, in *Là-Bas*, writing a biography of the medieval demonist and murderer Gilles de Rais, discovers the remnants of satanic practices still extant in France thanks to the guidance of Madame Chantelouve, who is reputed to have been visited by incubi and who seduces him. His friend, the sceptical medical man Des Hermies, meditates on the relationship between the possession cases of old and the hystero-epileptics of the present day. The materialists, he notes, have taken the trouble to revise the accounts of the sorcery trials of old, in which they found the symptoms of hysteria, and contrasts this with the appalling effrontery of the positivists, who

> lay everything at the account of major hysteria and they don't even know what this frightful malady is and what are its causes. No doubt Charcot determines very well the phases of the attack, notes the nonsensical and passional attitudes, the contortionist movements; he discovers hysterogenetic zones and can, by skilfully manipulating the ovaries, arrest or accelerate the crises, but as for forseeing them and learning the sources and the motives and curing them, that's another thing. Science goes all to pieces on the question of this inexplicable, stupefying malady, which consequently, is subject to the most diversified interpretations. . . .[27]

Even if the surrealists did not seriously entertain the validity of demonic possession, they shared Des Hermies' radical scepticism at the adequacy of a purely scientific solution and would have understood if not shared Durtal's ironic response to Des Hermies: ' "Mmmm," said Durtal, "since anything can be maintained and nothing is certain, succubacy has it. Basically it is more literary – and cleaner than positivism." ' That succubacy was regarded as a poetic manifestation of symptoms later defined as 'hysterical' is confirmed both in 'Le cinquantenaire de l'hystérie' and in Aragon's 'L'entrée des succubes'. It was both an underground form of acknowledging the primacy of hysteria in Freud's early analyses of sexuality – which regard hysteria as a largely but not exclusively female neurosis of social origins – and of rejecting the therapeutic claims of psychoanalysis.

Breton and Aragon, in the text accompanying photographs of the *attitudes passionnelles* of Charcot's patient Augustine in La Salpêtrière, reproduced in the same issue of *La révolution surréaliste* as the 'Recherches', take a starting point similar to Des Hermies, and, performing as 'rigorous theoreticians', examine the previous history of attempts to define hysteria (paying homage to both Charcot and Madame Chantelouve), which they see as alternating dialectically between diabolism and science. Arguing that its current definition as a pathological state is only a 'moment in the evolution of hysteria,' Breton and Aragon offer their own:

> Hysteria is a more or less irreducible mental state characterised by the subversion of the connections obtaining between the subject and the world of values to which he is practically supposed to belong: a subversion that occurs independently of any delusional system. This mental state is based on the reciprocal need for seduction, which explains the miracles hastily ascribed to medical suggestion (or counter-suggestion). Hysteria is not a pathological phenomenon and may in all respects be considered a supreme means of expression.[28]

Succubacy, therefore, as a residue via Romanticism of the medieval belief in possession, provided the surrealists with a poetic alibi and simultaneously functioned as a challenge to the psychiatric reduction of 'hysteria' to a pathological state. These figures emerge from the night world of sexuality – a hidden continuum of solitary and lost caresses and desires, as Aragon describes it in 'Entrée des succubes' – over which the waking mind has no control. It is not difficult to find here an analogy for the psychoanalysts' own arena, for in a sense the surrealists 'manifested a clandestine, nocturnal and "accursed" vision of the doctrines it defended'.[29] Just as their spiritism 'was more like a strident demonstration of iconoclasm than an appeal to the crystal ball', so their diabolism was the occasion for the assertion of the primacy of sexuality rather than abandon to the 'black tide' of occultism – but on their own terms, and not on those of either Freud or of the French psychoanalytical school.

Admittedly, the surrealists chose to ignore the distress of victims of hysteria, or the fact that it was analysed as a symptom of repressed sexual feelings, often of bisexual inclinations. Great – and acknowledged – though their debt to Freud was, they had to keep their distance from the practice of psychoanalysis, from the institutionalisation of a discipline. It could not be a part of their project to accept as given Freud's ideas in toto; a full account of their long and tortuous relation with the founder of psychoanalysis has still to be written, as has the sibling relationship with Lacan. It could be that surrealism almost more than any other modern movement created the conditions which have made it possible for languages of sexuality and the body to take form which have both provided the tools for a critique of surrealism from within and without and resisted the totalising accounts of other schools.

Notes

First Session

1. Crossed out: [(*Laughs*) Why ask me first? (He reads the question again)]
2. Crossed out: [I would like to intervene.]
3. Crossed out: [unusual to say the least]
4. [ANDRÉ BRETON I object most violently. (Péret [and] Unik then agree).]
5. [To give examples: I would cite M. (Max Jacob) and J. Cocteau.]
6. [Jean] *Trans.* Jean Lorrain was the pseudonym of Paul Duval (1856–1906), a minor symbolist poet and literary journalist. Quite rarely for the time, he had the courage to affirm his homosexuality proudly and publicly.
7. Crossed out: [But, for example, the books of Proust, typically, are to me the expression of this shortcoming.]
8. Crossed out: [I can even conceive of it not being practised.]
9. [(*Violently*.) It has nothing in common with homosexuality!]
10. According to the *Petit Larousse illustré*, 1980 edition, an 'incubus' is a 'male demon who takes advantage of women while they sleep', a 'succubus', a 'female demon who, according to tradition, seduces men while they sleep'. Both kinds come up again in subsequent sessions. *La Révolution surréaliste*, no.6 (1 March 1926) contains a text by Aragon entitled 'Entrance of the succubi'.
11. [What is the nature of the distinction you make between images of women with succubi and images of women]
12. [of two men masturbating and sucking each other in bed without penetration]
13. [I am absolutely in favour of it.]
14. [*General agreement.*]
15. Crossed out:[ANDRÉ BRETON Because that would be vulgar.
BENJAMIN PÉRET I protest.]
16. [I have a literary idea of it.] *Trans.* Simon-Théodore Jouffroy (1796–1843) was a spiritualist philosopher and lecturer at the École Normale Supérieure and the Sorbonne.

17. [The man and woman lying on their sides, legs entwined, the woman sitting astride the man, sodomy, sixty-nine.]

18. [Yes, I have a great taste for women's legs and feet.
RAYMOND QUENEAU For objects?
BENJAMIN PÉRET No, not particularly.]

19. [I didn't learn anything new.]

20. [It's not even enough, there could be more.] Crossed out: [ANDRÉ BRETON That's collectivism!]

21. [I can't think of any positive conditions.]

22. *Trans.* There is no English equivalent for a *frôleuse* or for *frôlement* in the senses they have here. *Frôlement*, from the verb *frôler*, is the action of lightly rubbing or brushing against something. A *frôleur* can mean a man with a mania for touching women; a *frôleuse* often simply means a temptress. The 'Lexique succinct de l'érotisme' included in the catalogue to the 1959 International Exhibition of Surrealism (see Appendix VI) gives a more specific definition, which seems appropriate here: '*Frôleuse* – an expert in seduction through surreptitious physical contact which seems more or less unintentional.' José Pierre suggests that this technique may have been one used by street prostitutes at the time.

23. [JACQUES PRÉVERT It makes me laugh.]

24. Crossed out: [PIERRE UNIK I hadn't understood what you meant by *frôleuse*. I withdraw my answer. I cannot love a *frôleuse*.]

25. [RAYMOND QUENEAU On the contrary.]

26. Crossed out: [You don't have to speak to do it.]

27. Crossed out: [RAYMOND QUENEAU Quite odious.]

Second Session

1. [Applied by me in a proportion of 75 per cent – 25 per cent by the woman. In terms of the restraints we impose on ourselves to achieve simultaneity, 75 per cent of the time it's self-restraint on my part.]

2. [ANDRÉ BRETON Very desirable?
MARCEL DUHAMEL Yes. In all this, something which is a very important factor for me is habit. The first time you make love with a woman it's very desirable but very difficult.
LOUIS ARAGON We must answer these questions quickly.]

3. [JACQUES–A. BOIFFARD 50 per cent.
ANDRÉ BRETON 50 per cent using artificial methods?
JACQUES–A. BOIFFARD Yes.
ANDRÉ BRETON Without them?
JACQUES–A. BOIFFARD Very rarely. The figures don't mean anything. Sometimes it's desirable, sometimes it isn't. Not always.]

4. [PIERRE UNIK Breton said just now it's a moral question. With respect to what?
ANDRÉ BRETON With respect to the methods used. Such methods are libertinism.]

5. [ANDRÉ BRETON For what reason?
GEORGES SADOUL It's more or less a matter of vocabulary.]

6. [or 85 per cent]

7. [ANDRÉ BRETON A fortiori, therefore, if the performance has been successful.]

8. [EVERYONE ELSE Yes.]

9. [For me, these would not be pathological cases.] It is important to underline this serious contradiction between the manuscript text (although it was corrected by Breton) and the text in *La révolution surréaliste*. Since, as far as I know, Breton never objected to it, it is the printed version which must be taken as correct. (*José Pierre*)

10. [General approval, with the exception of Breton, Baron, Duhamel and Péret, who protest.]

11. [LOUIS ARAGON Does anyone want to speak on this subject?]

12. [Does no one have an opinion on this subject?]

13. *Trans.* There is no equivalent in Britain for the French *droguerie*, which I've translated as 'household store' and which is sometimes more misleadingly translated as 'hardware shop'. The *droguerie* sells non-prescription medicines and toiletries as well as general household goods. A *pharmacie* (chemist) sells *only* medicines.

14. [I'm neither one nor the other.]

15. Crossed out: [except where it serves a very elevated notion of love]

16. The ellipses here are in the manuscript.

Third Session

1. Crossed out: [MARCEL NOLL Breton, same question.
ANDRÉ BRETON Naturally I wouldn't let myself be seen in such apparel for anything in the world.]

2. Crossed out: [I am entirely in favour in every case.]

3. Crossed out: [If the woman wants to do it.]

4. There follows a fairly long passage – a reply from Péret, it would seem – which has been particularly heavily crossed out.

5. Crossed out: [LOUIS ARAGON Would you like to tell us where that intuition comes from?]

6. Breton has added a note to the manuscript here, preceded by an asterisk: 'Punctumcœcum (circumf. and centre).'

7. These ellipses are followed by a veritable thicket of crossings-out.

Fourth Session

1. As José Pierre points out in his own footnote at this point in the French edition, readers need to know something about Jean Genbach (whose real name was Ernest de Gengenbach) to understand this session. In his *History of Surrealism* (Pelican, Harmondsworth 1973), Maurice Nadeau provides a useful summary of Genbach's strange career, which is worth quoting here:

> A Jesuit Abbé, he had fallen in love with an actress at the Odéon and in her company frequented restaurants and dance-halls. Defrocked by his bishop, he had lost his

mistress, who loved him only in his cassock, and happened to pick up an issue of *La révolution surréaliste* at the moment he was thinking of suicide. Hence he did not fling himself into the Gérardmer lake as he had planned, but entered into relations with Breton and his friends. He was to be seen at the Dôme or the Rotonde, a flower in the buttonhole of his soutane, which he had begun wearing again as a provocation, a woman on his lap, vilified by the respectable passers-by whom he delighted in scandalising. He divided his time between a scabrous worldly life, periods of calm with a Russian woman, an artist, in Clamart, and retreats at the Abbey of Solesmes. When there were rumours that the prodigal was about to return to the bosom of the Church, Gengenbach enlightened the surrealists in a letter to Breton:

'It is my custom to go several times a year to rest and recover my spirits with the monks . . . and the surrealist circle is well aware of my pronounced taste for escapades in monasteries. . . . As for the ecclesiastical habit, I wear it by caprice for the moment, because my suit is torn. . . . I also find it affords me certain advantages in initiating sadistic relations with the American women who pick me up in the Bois at night. . . .

'I have found *no solution*, no escape, no pragmatism that is acceptable. There remains my faith in Christ, cigarettes, and the jazz records I love – "Tea for Two", "Yearning" – and above all, there remains *surrealism*.'

This curious individual was to end badly all the same. Trying to reconcile Christianity and surrealism, after writing such works as *Judas ou le Vampire surréaliste* (Aigle noir, Paris 1930) and *Satan en Espagne*, he denounced Breton as the living incarnation of Lucifer and the surrealists as 'conscious demoniac victims of possession or demons incarnate'. Exorcism, he added, was 'unfortunately relegated to the remote Middle Ages', but he nursed hopes that 'suffering and the vicissitudes of life would fling these conquistadors of Hell at the foot of the Cross'. Unfortunately, 'no theologian's argument will convince a surrealist, only the love of some passionately desired female saint can transform a surrealist'. (trans. Richard Howard)

2. The ellipses here follow the manuscript text.
3. As above.
4. The word in square brackets has been added to make sense of the phrase.
5. The manuscript tells us no more about Bataille's idea.
6. Crossed out: [PIERRE UNIK I cannot see any moral hope except in chastity.]
7. *Trans.* Breton is referring to 'Le rideau cramoisi', one of the stories in Barbey d'Aurevilly's *Les Diaboliques* (1874). In the story, an officer staying at a country house is seduced by a mysterious young woman. Their relationship is purely sexual. At the end of a particularly torrid night with her, he discovers that he has been making love with a corpse.

Fifth Session

1. This participant, who is only given an initial and only intervenes once, may perhaps be Max Morise.
2. The sentence is incomplete in the manuscript. Perhaps Breton means that

Unik's earlier exclusion from the discussion should be terminated if he accepts this condition.

3. *Trans.* Georges Carpentier, a famous French boxer of the period.
4. Ellipsis as in the manuscript.
5. It is not possible to identify this 'friend'.
6. The question mark in brackets corresponds to the manuscript text.
7. Crossed out: [RAYMOND QUENEAU In that case, we're not talking about life. MARCEL NOLL Surrealism has never been anything other than a meaning of life.]
8. Prévert means that he is supporting Queneau's position.
9. Crossed out: [Shove Dada up your arse.]
10. Crossed out: [Great disgust.]

Sixth Session

1. Perhaps it should be 'physical' here. But the manuscript unmistakably has 'psychological'.
2. Crossed out: [I protest most strongly at this answer.]

Seventh Session

1. The participation of Boiffard is uncertain. In the list of participants, 'Bo' seems as if it can only refer to him. But in the actual discussion, the only intervention by this 'Bo' has been completely crossed out. We know that Boiffard was to be a very active collaborator on *Documents* with Bataille from December 1929. *Trans.*: *Documents*, which lasted for fifteen issues, was a journal which regrouped a number of former surrealists, including Robert Desnos, Michel Leiris, André Masson and Roger Vitrac. It was partly in response to Bataille's positions, developed in *Documents*, that Breton wrote his *Second Manifesto of Surrealism*.
2. Given her comments on 'possession' (p.103) it seems very likely that Y. is a woman.
3. In his autobiography, *Raconte pas ta vie* (Paris 1972), Marcel Duhamel faithfully repeats – from memory – Jean Baldensperger's account of his zoophiliac experience.
4. Deleted: (BO These sexual jokes make me laugh often enough, because they probably correspond to things which I have repressed; there is also a degree of embarassment.)
5. *Trans.* The French for a female donkey is *une ânesse.*

Eighth Session

1. Crossed out: [Are these representations linked to childhood memories?]
2. The word *empêchement* (impediment) is unclear in the manuscript.

Ninth Session

1. The participation of this 'Bauer' is conjectural: he only intervenes once in the discussion.
2. The manuscript does not specify who asks this question.
3. Eluard is referring to his wife, Gala, who at this time had been living with Salvador Dali for more than a year.
4. There is nothing to indicate what this series of vowels might mean. *Trans.*: But the French pronunciation of them might be approximately represented as follows: 'Ah! Oh! Ee!'

Tenth Session

1. *Sic.*
2. This word has been derived from an ambiguous abbreviation in the manuscript.
3. Crossed out: [Love tends to remain a bolt from the blue. You are subordinating love to desire.]

Eleventh Session

1. *Trans.* Giorgio Baffo, a Venetian nobleman (1694–1768), was, according to Apollinaire, 'the greatest priapic poet who ever lived.' More recently, his work has been celebrated by the surrealist writer André Pieyre de Mandiargues.
2. In the manuscript, Breton has added: '(This is not true) (Second reading)', then: 'This is absolutely untrue, third reading, but I would like to.'
3. *Trans.* Unik is presumably referring to the prolific and popular comic writer, Georges Courteline (1861–1929). But the allusion is just a part of the banter that predominates in this session, as is the one to Molière which precedes it, where Breton is simply mocking Unik for sounding sententious ('The ear is made for the tongue, not for the cock.').

Twelfth Session

1. Crossed out: 'The arse.'
2. There is no indication as to what this mysterious '+ . . . ' might mean.

Appendix II

1. Published in *La révolution surréaliste*, no. 12, 15 December 1929. In volume one of André Breton's *Œuvres complètes* (Bibliothèque de la Pléiade, Gallimard, Paris 1988),

p. 1759, Marguerite Bonnet confirms that the text of this inquiry was written by André Breton.

2. Among the responses to this inquiry was Magritte's famous painting representing a naked woman with the inscription: 'I do not see the [. . .] hidden in the forest', surrounded by the photographs of sixteen surrealists with their eyes closed.

Appendix III

1. *Minotaure*, no. 3-4, December 1933. The comments are by André Breton, who included them in *L'amour fou* in 1937 (where they formed most of the second section of the book), prefaced by the following remarks: 'It was with these words that Paul Eluard and I not long ago instigated an inquiry whose results were published in the journal *Minotaure*. When we published the responses, I felt the need to specify the meaning of the two questions and to draw some preliminary conclusions from the views expressed.'

2. This quotation accompanied a drawing by Man Ray – placed above the inquiry's title – which faithfully illustrated Lautréamont's phrase. Neither the drawing nor the quotation were included in *L'amour fou*.

3. *Trans.* Antoine-Augustin Cournot (1801–77), mathematician, economist and philosopher of *probabilisme*.

4. *Trans.* Henri Poincaré (1856–1912), mathematician and philosopher, whose studies of science were relatively popular. His cousin, Raymond, was a president of the Third Republic.

5. This is in fact the first time Breton defined *objective chance*.

Appendix IV

1. First published in *Le surréalisme, même*, nos 4 and 5, Spring 1958 and Spring 1959.

Appendix V

1. The text of this inquiry was published in *La brèche, action surréaliste* no. 6, June 1964; the responses in no. 7, December 1964, and no. 8, November 1965.

2. This was followed by the instruction: 'Address your response to Vincent Bounoure, 49, boulevard de la Gare, Paris (13e).'

Appendix VI

1. The International Surrealist Exhibition, devoted to eroticism, opened on 15 December 1959, at the Galerie Daniel Cordier, rue de Miromesnil, Paris 8, and closed

at the end of February 1960. The two texts here were republished in *Le surréalisme et la peinture* (Gallimard, Paris 1965), set in two parallel columns as they were in the exhibition catalogue. Here we have printed them one after the other.

Afterword

1. Maurice Nadeau, *The History of Surrealism*, Collier Books, New York 1967, p. 143.
2. Louis Aragon, 'Introduction à 1930', *La révolution surréaliste*, no. 12, 15 December 1929, p. 62.
3. Ibid.
4. Such 'inquiries' or surveys were popular at the time, and many journals, both avant-garde and conservative, ran them on a variety of topics. Unlike the surrrealist 'Recherches', though, which were restricted to the more or less closed circle of the surrealists themselves, the 'Inquiry' of 1929 was widely circulated. Responses from *Commœdia, Paris-Midi*, and even some derisory comments from the reactionary *Action française* were published in *La révolution surréaliste*, as well as replies from the surrealists themselves and from such prominent figures as Roch Grey. Answers covered a wide spectrum of opinion. This was in fact quite deliberate, and is a part of the dialectical relationship between the 'Recherches' and the 'Enquête'. If the 'Recherches' accepted no definition of love and/or sexuality as given, the 'Enquête appeared to start from a position of an absolute belief in love and proceeded to ask qustions that then problematised this in relation to the social and political spheres.
5. André Breton, *Manifestoes of Surrealism*, trans. Richard Seaver and Helen R. Lane, Ann Arbor 1972, p. 10.
6. André Breton, *L'un dans l'autre*, Paris 1970, p. 7.
7. *Nadja* chronicles Breton's friendship with a woman whose precarious hold on reality was one of the chief causes of her fascination for him; the mystery in their relationship was not that of the magical reciprocity of love, but rather that of repeated chance encounters and coincidences located more within the experience of the streets of Paris than in that of the body. Nadja eventually goes mad and is incarcerated, and this is the occasion of an outspoken attack by Breton on mental institutions.
8. Walter Benjamin, 'Surrealism: Last Snapshot of the European Intelligentsia', in *One-Way Street*, New Left Books, London 1979, p. 237.
9. Breton, *Manifestoes*, p. 177.
10. Benjamin, 'Surrealism', p. 277.
11. André Breton, 'Second manifeste du surréalisme', *R.S.* 12, pp. 2-3 (translation based in part on Breton, *Manifestoes*).
12. In *Le surréalisme au service de la révolution*, no. 4, 1931.
13. Whitney Chadwick quotes the following passage from the English surrealist painter Ithell Colquhoun's 'The Water Stone of the Wise', which rejects the Oedipal myth rather on grounds of its incarnation of sexual difference: 'Oedipus will be king no longer but will return to Colonus. The new myth, the myth of the Siamese Twins, will make of him a forgotten bogey.' *Women Artists and the Surrealist Movement*, Thames and Hudson, London 1985, p. 105.
14. Sigmund Freud, 'The Sexual Aberrations' (from *Three Essays on Sexuality*), in

Freud on Women: A Reader, ed. Elisabeth Young-Bruhl, Norton, New York and London 1990, p. 90.

15. *Freud on Women*, p. 45.

16. Aragon, 'Introduction à 1930', p. 64.

17. Chadwick records from an interview with Leonora Carrington the following splendid statement: 'In *l'amour passion*, it is the loved one, the other, who gives the key. Now the question is: Who can the loved one be? It can be a man or a horse or another woman' (*Women Artists*, p. 105). Such remarks by the women associated with the surrealist group are not uncommon.

18. Guy Rosolato, 'Le fétishisme', in *Le désir et la perversion* as quoted by Xavière Gauthier, *Surréalisme et sexualité*, Gallimard, Paris 1971, p. 357.

19. Gauthier, *Surréalisme et sexualité*, p. 331.

20. Susan Rubin Suleiman, *Subversive Intent: Gender, Politics and the Avant-Garde*, Harvard University Press, Cambridge 1990, p. 19.

21. In *L'Amour Fou: Photography and Surrealism*, Abbeville, New York 1985.

22. See for instance Rudolf Kuenzli, 'Surrealism and Misogyny', in *Surrealism and Women*, ed. Mary Ann Caws, Rudolf Kuenzli and Gwen Raaberg, MIT Press, Cambridge (Mass.) 1991.

23. Georges Bataille, 'Le langage des fleurs', *Documents*, Paris 1929. See my 'Documents', in *Dada and Surrealism Reviewed*, Arts Council of Great Britain, London 1978.

24. Elisabeth Roudinesco, *Jacques Lacan and Co.*, University of Chicago Press 1990, p. 17. The *Revue française de psychanalyse* began publication in 1927.

25. Gauthier, *Surréalisme et sexualité*, p. 51.

26. This is a standard dictionary definition, and similar terms are used for the (male) incubus. It is interesting, however, that the *Larousse du XXième siècle* genders the 'commerce' between human and succubus/incubus differently: the succubus in this version takes the form of a woman 'in order to submit to the man', while the incubus is a 'sort of demon which abuses of women as they sleep'. This passivising of the succubus runs counter to the surrealists' idea, which took pleasure in the active nature of the succubus.

27. J.-K. Huysmans, *Down There* (*Là-Bas*), New York 1924, pp. 153-4.

28. 'Le cinquantenaire de l'hystérie', *R.S.* 11, p. 22. It is interesting that the first issue of the *Revue française de psychanalyse* for 1928, its second year of publication, printed the translation of Freud's famous case study of the hysteric 'Dora', the (incomplete) analysis of a young girl whose gynecophilic feelings for her father's mistress lay at the root of her illness. Whether this moment was chosen to publish also in homage to Charcot is unclear.

29. Roudinesco, *Lacan*.